Schraff, Anne E.

Marcus Garvey

MARCUS
GARVEY

The African-American Biographies Series

MARIAN ANDERSON
Singer and Humanitarian
0-7660-1211-5

LOUIS ARMSTRONG
King of Jazz
0-89490-997-5

BENJAMIN BANNEKER
Astronomer and Mathematician
0-7660-1208-5

MARY MCLEOD BETHUNE
Educator and Activist
0-7660-1771-0

JULIAN BOND
Civil Rights Activist and Chairman of
the NAACP
0-7660-1549-1

RALPH BUNCHE
Winner of the Nobel Peace Prize
0-7660-1203-4

GEORGE WASHINGTON CARVER
Scientist and Inventor
0-7660-1770-2

BESSIE COLEMAN
First Black Woman Pilot
0-7660-1545-9

FREDERICK DOUGLASS
Speaking Out Against Slavery
0-7660-1773-7

DR. CHARLES DREW
Blood Bank Innovator
0-7660-2117-3

W. E. B. DU BOIS
Champion of Civil Rights
0-7660-1209-3

PAUL LAURENCE DUNBAR
Portrait of a Poet
0-7660-1350-2

DUKE ELLINGTON
Giant of Jazz
0-89490-691-7

MARCUS GARVEY
Controversial Champion
of Black Pride
0-7660-2168-8

NIKKI GIOVANNI
Poet of the People
0-7660-1238-7

WHOOPI GOLDBERG
Comedian and Movie Star
0-7660-1205-0

FANNIE LOU HAMER
Fighting for the Right to Vote
0-7660-1772-9

LORRAINE HANSBERRY
Playwright and Voice of Justice
0-89490-945-2

MATTHEW HENSON
Co-Discoverer of the North Pole
0-7660-1546-7

LANGSTON HUGHES
Poet of the Harlem Renaissance
0-89490-815-4

ZORA NEALE HURSTON
Southern Storyteller
0-89490-685-2

JESSE JACKSON
Civil Rights Activist
0-7660-1390-1

MAHALIA JACKSON
The Voice of Gospel and Civil Rights
0-7660-2115-7

QUINCY JONES
Musician, Composer, Producer
0-89490-814-6

BARBARA JORDAN
Congresswoman, Lawyer,
Educator
0-89490-692-5

CORETTA SCOTT KING
Striving for Civil Rights
0-89490-811-1

MARTIN LUTHER KING, JR.
Leader for Civil Rights
0-89490-687-9

JOHN LEWIS
From Freedom Rider to Congressman
0-7660-1768-0

THURGOOD MARSHALL
Civil Rights Attorney and
Supreme Court Justice
0-7660-1547-5

KWEISI MFUME
Congressman and NAACP Leader
0-7660-1237-9

TONI MORRISON
Nobel Prize-Winning Author
0-89490-688-7

WALTER DEAN MYERS
Writer for Real Teens
0-7660-1206-9

JESSE OWENS
Track and Field Legend
0-89490-812-X

COLIN POWELL
Soldier and Patriot
0-89490-810-3

A. PHILIP RANDOLPH
Union Leader and Civil Rights
Crusader
0-7660-1544-0

PAUL ROBESON
Actor, Singer, Political Activist
0-89490-944-4

JACKIE ROBINSON
Baseball's Civil Rights Legend
0-89490-690-9

WILMA RUDOLPH
The Greatest Woman Sprinter
in History
0-7660-2291-9

BETTY SHABAZZ
Sharing the Vision
of Malcolm X
0-7660-1210-7

MARY CHURCH TERRELL
Speaking Out for Civil Rights
0-7660-2116-5

HARRIET TUBMAN
Moses of the Underground Railroad
0-7660-1548-3

MADAM C. J. WALKER
Self-Made Businesswoman
0-7660-1204-2

DENZEL WASHINGTON
Academy Award–Winning Actor
0-7660-2131-9

IDA B. WELLS-BARNETT
Crusader Against Lynching
0-89490-947-9

CARTER G. WOODSON
Father of African-American History
0-89490-946-0

RICHARD WRIGHT
Author of *Native Son* and *Black Boy*
0-7660-1769-9

—African-American Biographies—

MARCUS GARVEY

Controversial Champion of Black Pride

Series Consultant:
Dr. Russell L. Adams, Chairman
Department of Afro-American Studies, Howard University

Anne Schraff

Enslow Publishers, Inc.

40 Industrial Road	PO Box 38
Box 398	Aldershot
Berkeley Heights, NJ 07922	Hants GU12 6BP
USA	UK

http://www.enslow.com

Library of Congress Cataloging-in-Publication Data

Schraff, Anne E.
　　Marcus Garvey : controversial champion of black pride / Anne Schraff.
　　　　p. cm. — (African-American biographies)
　　Summary: Chronicles the life of Marcus Garvey, a fiery black leader who began a crusade for African Americans to fight against oppression in the early years of the twentieth century.
　　Includes bibliographical references and index.
　　ISBN 0-7660-2168-8
　　　　1. Garvey, Marcus, 1887–1940—Juvenile literature. 2. African Americans—Biography—Juvenile literature. 3. Jamaican Americans—Biography—Juvenile literature. 4. Civil rights workers—United States—Biography—Juvenile literature. 5. Intellectuals—United States—Biography—Juvenile literature. 6. Universal Negro Improvement Association—Juvenile literature. 7. African Americans—Civil rights—History—20th century—Juvenile literature. 8. United States—Race relations—Juvenile literature. [1. Garvey, Marcus, 1887–1940. 2. Civil rights workers. 3. African Americans—Biography. 4. Universal Negro Improvement Association.] I. Title. II. Series.
　　E185.97.G3S37 2004
　　305.896′073′0092—dc21
　　　　　　　　　　　　　　　　　　　　　　2003008512

Printed in the United States of America

10 9 8 7 6 5 4 3 2 1

To Our Readers:
We have done our best to make sure all Internet Addresses in this book were active and appropriate when we went to press. However, the author and the publisher have no control over and assume no liability for the material available on those Internet sites or on other Web sites they may link to. Any comments or suggestions can be sent by e-mail to comments@enslow.com or to the address on the back cover.

Every effort has been made to locate all copyright holders of material used in this book. If any errors or omissions have occurred, corrections will be made in future editions of this book.

Illustration Credits: Clipart.com, p. 12; Courtesy of © The Mariners' Museum, Newport News, Virginia, pp. 54, 60; Library of Congress, pp. 6, 15, 23, 26, 28, 35, 41, 49, 57, 65, 68, 72, 75, 80, 95, 108, 110; Marcus Garvey Portrait Collection, Photographs and Prints Division, Schomburg Center for Research in Black Culture, The New York Public Library, Astor, Lenox and Tilden Foundations, pp. 83, 101, 112; Xavier University Archives and Special Collections, New Orleans, p. 97.

Cover Illustration: Library of Congress

Contents

Marcus Garvey

1

"NO MORE FEAR"

wenty-eight-year-old Marcus Garvey had been working in his Jamaican homeland to improve conditions for black laborers. He had also traveled to Central and South America to promote the rights of underpaid workers from the islands of the West Indies. In the spring of 1916, he arrived in the United States, seeking support and money to fund his political activities. There was a large West Indian population in New York City.

Even before coming to the United States, Garvey had read about American race riots that were causing death and destruction across the country. Tensions between blacks and whites were growing. Then, in July 1917, in East St. Louis, Illinois, the worst race riot in United States history broke out. Garvey read the newspaper accounts about it.

The trouble erupted after a rumor spread that a white man had been shot by a black robber. Tensions had already been running high in this railroad and factory town. Black workers from the Deep South were moving in by the thousands. Whites resented the competition for jobs. Any rumor of a black-on-white crime sent angry white mobs into black neighborhoods to beat people and burn houses.

Plumes of smoke rose into the mid-afternoon sky as flames licked at rows of frame houses. White rioters cut fire hoses with axes, leaving the hoses useless against the inferno ravaging the black neighborhood. Firefighters watched helplessly as block after block turned to ashes. Men, women, and children fled their burning homes only to be attacked with fists and guns by a fierce white mob.

Before National Guardsmen brought the riots under control, more than three hundred black homes and businesses had been burned to the ground. Eight white people and thirty-nine black people had been killed. Hundreds of black families fled East St. Louis never to return.[1]

Two years later, in July 1919, fifteen white people and twenty-three black people were killed in a race riot in Chicago. A thousand black families were left homeless.

The race riots had broken out because of changes in the community. Black people were beginning to get jobs and improve their status. Seeing this made local whites angry and frightened. In return, blacks were enraged at whites who were trying to deny them their basic right—to work and to pursue the American dream of a better life.

Marcus Garvey denounced all the riots. He saw in the angry mood of blacks a chance to launch his movement to lift black people up. He wanted to unite them into an organization strong enough to demand and gain equality in working conditions and salaries. Garvey said that for three hundred years black people had "given their life blood" to help build America, and they deserved better than to be burned out of their homes.[2]

In public speeches and newspapers, the passionate young man bitterly criticized the laws that kept thousands of black soldiers in segregated units in the battles of World War I. Although racial segregation was widespread throughout American society, the segregation of soldiers who were fighting for their country was especially offensive. Garvey warned darkly that the next time black soldiers took up arms, it might not be for the defense of the United States—it might be in their own defense.[3]

Although some black leaders were looking for compromise with white America, Garvey shouted defiance. "I am the equal of any white man," he proclaimed to the black crowds who had begun to gather around him. "I want you to feel the same way. No more fear. No more cringing."[4]

Garvey wanted black Americans to demand good jobs and housing, the right to join unions, the right to vote in the South, and the right to use public accommodations such as buses and rest rooms. "Up, you mighty race," he cried.[5]

From the ashes of East St. Louis to the crowded cities of the North, hundreds, then thousands, came to listen to Marcus Garvey. He electrified his audiences as he began a crusade that was to establish him as one of the most fervent and controversial black leaders of the twentieth century.

2

JAMAICAN CHILD

arcus Mosiah Garvey was born on August 17, 1887, in Saint Ann's Bay, a village on the northwestern coast of Jamaica. He was the eleventh child of Sarah and Marcus Garvey. Only Marcus and his older sister, Indiana, survived to adulthood. The others died in infancy or early childhood.

Marcus was named for his father, a dignified, intelligent man who worked as a stonemason. He cut and shaped Jamaica's white rock for use in building large plantation homes. Although slavery had been

Marcus Garvey grew up in Jamaica, which was ruled by the British government.

abolished in Jamaica in 1883, the better homes were still occupied by white people.

Marcus later recalled his father as "a man of brilliant intellect and dashing courage" who was also "severe, firm, determined and strong."[1] Marcus's father loved books and had a large library. Other residents of the neighborhood called him Mr. Garvey and thought him out of place in the working-class town.[2] His reputation as a learned man led many neighbors to seek his advice for legal and business problems.

Marcus Garvey, Sr., was known as a stubborn man who would not yield when he thought he was right. At one time, he began receiving a daily newspaper that he had not ordered. He decided it was a gift from the publisher. Later, when the publisher tried to collect for the papers, Garvey refused to give him any money. The publisher took him to court, where Garvey was ordered to pay. Still Garvey refused, and as a result he lost part of his property. In later disputes with neighbors over property lines, Garvey lost more land. Finally, he was left with only the land his house was sitting on. Marcus Garvey, Jr., later lamented that although his father "once had a fortune; he died poor."[3]

Marcus's father believed he had descended from black slaves held by the Spanish. Spaniards had occupied Jamaica from the time Christopher Columbus arrived in 1494 until the British conquered it in 1655. After the British occupation, the slaves seized their freedom and fled into the hills. They courageously resisted all efforts to return them to slavery. They became known as Maroons.[4]

Sarah Jane Richards Garvey, Marcus's mother, was a beautiful, gentle woman. Her son later said of her, "My mother was a sober and conscientious Christian, too soft and good for the time in which she lived."[5]

Sarah Garvey came from a Jamaican farm family. She and her brother owned a plot of land, where they cultivated citrus and allspice trees. Allspice berries are used for seasoning. A medicine also comes from this tree. Sarah added to the family income by making and selling cakes and other pastries. She was, according to her son, "always willing to return a smile for a blow."[6] When someone was unkind to her, she did not strike back.

Young Marcus was nicknamed Moses from his middle name, Mosiah. As a child, he harvested fruit from his mother's trees, which were not far from the family home. In his spare time, he rode a bicycle and swam in the bay. Both his parents valued learning, and the boy spent many hours reading in his father's library.

Years later, Marcus Garvey, Jr., recalled his education as coming from "many sources," including "private tutors, two public schools, two grammar or high schools and two colleges."[7]

The Garvey land adjoined the land of two white families. As a child, Marcus played freely with his white neighbors and was not aware of racial prejudice. He enjoyed a special friendship with a white girl his own age, and he later remembered, "We were two innocent fools who never dreamed of a race feeling and problem."[8] But when the girl turned fourteen, her parents forbade her to continue the friendship with Marcus.

All the white playmates of his childhood—the friends who had shared swimming, racing, and

Many black Jamaicans were laborers on large plantations owned by whites. The families above lived and worked on a tobacco plantation.

biking—ended the relationship when they became teenagers. It was understood that only as young children could whites and blacks be companions. As teenagers, they were not to mix. When this happened to Marcus, he understood for the first time that he was different. He later described himself as "annoyed" by the discovery.[9]

At the age of fourteen, in 1901, Marcus was apprenticed to his godfather, Alfred Ernest Burrowes, who ran a print shop in St. Ann's Bay. Marcus would learn how to be a printer. He was very efficient at his tasks, and he boasted, "I was strong and manly and I made them respect me."[10] Burrowes also had a large library, and Marcus used all his free time to read. He pored over magazines, newspapers, and books, often reading about foreign lands. Then he would sit on the wharf on the bay and watch the sailors loading ships. He dreamed of taking those ships to far-off lands when he was grown.

At seventeen, in 1904, Marcus became a journeyman printer at Port Maria in St. Mary's Parish. A journeyman is a craftsman who has finished his initial period of training—the apprenticeship—and can now work independently.

In 1906, Garvey moved to Kingston, the capital of Jamaica, to work at his uncle's printery, the P. A. Benjamin Manufacturing Company. To the teenage boy, Kingston was a bustling city. He loved going

downtown to listen to the public debates on Victoria
Pier. People argued about local problems and world
issues. Sometimes Marcus joined in the debates. He was
impressed by the oratory, and he was eager to learn how
to speak well himself. He attended barbershop forums
and park debates and listened closely to the different
styles of the speakers. Every Sunday he went to a
different church to carefully observe the speaking styles
of Kingston's most important ministers.

Marcus would go home after hearing others speak.
There he practiced by reading passages from books
aloud. He carried a pocket dictionary and was always
adding new words to his vocabulary. Soon Marcus began
appearing regularly on the debating circuit. He spoke
on all the important issues of the day. He organized
speaking contests for younger boys. He taught them
debating skills and urged them to improve themselves.
Later, he referred to this teaching as "uplift work."[11]

From a young age, Marcus believed that everybody
had the duty to lift up those further down on the ladder.
He believed that when someone develops a skill that
takes him or her higher in life, that person must reach
down and pull the next person up higher, too. It was
not good enough to be successful. A person had to help
others be successful too.

In 1907 Marcus was elected to the leadership of the
typesetters union. This new responsibility, along with
natural disasters and family problems, brought great

challenges to the young man's life. A serious earthquake and fire struck Jamaica, destroying the crops Marcus's parents depended upon. Sarah Garvey separated from her husband and moved to Kingston with Marcus. Marcus had always been closer to his mother than to his father. He described her as "the direct opposite of my father. He was severe."[12] Marcus's mother died in 1908, and he lost contact with his father. At twenty-one years old, he was on his own. The loss of his mother and the economic problems that the earthquake brought to Kingston weighed heavily on the young man.

Marcus was foreman at the print factory, responsible for seeing that the work got done. Because of the natural disasters, food was scarce in Kingston, and merchants charged outrageous prices. The black workers at the factory were paid less than their white counterparts and could not afford these higher prices on their small salaries. The black workers walked off the job. They went on strike, saying they would not return until they were given wages high enough to cover living expenses.

As a manager, Marcus was not expected to be part of the strike—but as a union leader, he was. He chose to stand with the strikers, supporting them in their demands. Marcus's employer offered him more money if he would not join the strike, but Marcus refused. He walked out with the other black workers. He was fired, as were all the other strikers. New workers were hired to take the jobs.

The government printing office soon hired Marcus, but he had been deeply affected by the strike. He later recalled, "I saw the injustice done to my race because it was black."[13] The idea was reinforced in his mind that black people were the victims of white oppression wherever the two races lived together.

Garvey became active in political clubs in Kingston. He discussed with other black men how they could fight against oppression. Garvey joined the National Club and became its assistant secretary. Many of the club members were lawyers who fought for the rights of black Jamaicans. Garvey read the club's newspaper, *Our Own,* and published his own newsletter, *Watchman.* Garvey's little newsletter did not last long, but it gave him good experience.

Marcus Garvey became determined to raise his voice on behalf of downtrodden black workers throughout the region. He needed money for his own support and for his cause, and economic conditions in Jamaica were not good. Many young black men were going to Central and South America to take jobs that paid far more than anything they could find in Jamaica. Garvey decided he would go as well. At twenty-three years old, Marcus Garvey, Jr., left Jamaica for the first time.

3

CENTRAL AMERICA AND LONDON

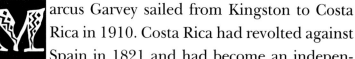

arcus Garvey sailed from Kingston to Costa
Rica in 1910. Costa Rica had revolted against
Spain in 1821 and had become an independent nation. But its economy was dominated by an
American company—United Fruit. Most of the people
in Costa Rica who had jobs worked for United Fruit,
which was one of the smaller American companies.
The economy of the nation depended on American
companies.

Garvey hoped to earn enough money in Costa Rica
to start a Jamaican organization for the improvement
of black life. Upon his arrival, he immediately secured

a job as a timekeeper at a large banana plantation owned by United Fruit. The timekeeper kept track of the hours worked by the laborers. The workers, who were mostly black, harvested the fruit and cleared uncultivated land for more planting. Garvey hoped to earn enough money to start his Jamaican organization for the improvement of black life.

Many West Indians in Costa Rica had difficult and dangerous jobs, such as draining swamps so that new orchards could be planted. The men were beset by poisonous snakes and deadly tropical illnesses. They worked long hours for low wages. Garvey was angered by the terrible working conditions and the meager pay, so he went to the British consulate to complain. Most of the workers were from West Indian countries and were therefore British subjects. Garvey thought the consulate would be interested in the workers' welfare. But he was wrong.

At the consulate at Puerto Limón in Costa Rica, Garvey was ignored. The British government, which was cooperating with United Fruit and the Costa Rican government, turned a blind eye to worker abuse. The high employment rate in Costa Rica was helpful to places like Jamaica, where jobs were hard to come by. None of the people in power wanted to upset the balance.

Garvey recalled that he came to a grim conclusion after being repeatedly ignored at British consulates.

He decided "that no white person would ever regard the life of a black man equal to that of a white man."[1] He concluded that if anyone was to help the black immigrants in Costa Rica and fight for their rights, it would have to be someone like him, a black man with a mission.

Garvey got a new job on the docks at Puerto Limón, and he started a newspaper to promote his ideas. *La Nacionale* (The Nation) was launched. Garvey hoped it would motivate black laborers to fight for their rights. But the paper failed without arousing much interest. In 1910, Garvey traveled to Nicaragua, Colombia, and Venezuela. Wherever he went, he saw West Indians struggling under the burden of hard work and low pay.

In Panama, Garvey found many immigrant blacks working on construction of a waterway across the Isthmus of Panama. The canal was a United States project to connect the Atlantic and Pacific Oceans. Once more, white laborers were earning more than blacks and were being given less dangerous assignments. From the tobacco fields and copper mines of Ecuador to the fields and orchards of Central America, Garvey saw West Indians being exploited. He repeatedly visited British consulates, pleading for more concern for their black British subjects. Over and over, he was told that Great Britain did not want to risk upsetting the status quo—the way things were.

These Costa Rican workers are cutting bananas from trees. Garvey was outraged at the poor working conditions he saw for blacks throughout Central America.

For almost two years, Garvey wandered around Latin America, trying to do something for exploited black workers, but he had no success. In 1911, he fell ill with malaria and was forced to return to Jamaica to recuperate. Although he was weary and frustrated, Garvey refused to give up his cause. After recovering his health, he began meeting with West Indian families whose husbands, brothers, and sons were employed in Central and South America. There, he was warmly received. Like Garvey, these families were worried about their loved ones in far-off places. Some had already lost a family member to work-related accidents and to disease. Garvey collected this information and showed it to the governor of Jamaica. He once again ran into a stone wall. The governor, like other British officials, knew that interfering with immigrant working conditions would be risky to the economies of the countries involved.

Garvey made a courageous decision. If he could get no satisfaction from local British authorities, he would appeal personally to the government in London. Garvey had very little money, though, and such a trip would be costly. He contacted his sister, Indiana, who was working as a nanny in London. She generously sent him the money, and Garvey set sail for Great Britain.

The twenty-five-year-old Garvey got a job as soon as he arrived in London, loading cargo on the docks.

At work, he met many West Indians and other blacks from around the world. Their stories further strengthened his belief in the need for reform. Garvey saw a pattern of abuse: Wherever black workers went, their rights were violated.

Garvey often visited the House of Commons. There he heard a famous British politician, Lloyd George, debating other powerful men. Garvey also made frequent trips to Hyde Park, where daily debates took place. Hyde Park reminded Garvey of his youth, when he had first listened to the debates at Victoria Pier. Occasionally, Garvey joined in debates that interested him. At this new podium, he talked about the struggles of the West Indian immigrants.

Garvey's thirst for knowledge led him to Birkbeck College in London, a school for working-class people without the time or funds to attend a regular college. The informal classes allowed students to come to class whenever they had some free time. Garvey studied law and philosophy, ancient Greek history, and the Greek philosophers Socrates and Plato. Later on, he would use the style of the Socratic dialogues to write about race problems in the world. The Socratic dialogues used questions and answers to bring out the truth of an issue. One voice asked an important question, and the second voice replied to it, much as in a play.

Garvey also learned about the rich history of black people. Before he came to London, all the

Hyde Park Corner in London, shown here in 1900, is a famous gathering place for spontaneous speeches and loud debates.

black-skinned people Garvey had met seemed to be oppressed and poor: laborers at the bottom of the heap. Now he read about black men who had ruled great, rich empires. Sunni Ali, warrior king of the African kingdom of Songhay, built a great canal and ruled more territory than Napoleon of France. Garvey also learned about Askia the Great, who also ruled Songhay and the fabled city of Timbuktu.

Garvey asked himself what had happened to his people. How could a proud, intelligent people have been reduced to slavery? In his frustration, Garvey began studying Pan-Africanism, the idea that all blacks of the world were one people with one common homeland: Africa. In past glories he saw hope for the future.

The great black American orator Frederick Douglass, who escaped from slavery before the Civil War, saw the dark-skinned pyramid builders of Egypt as the direct relatives of all Africans and other black people.[2] Similarly, Garvey would one day write, "This race of ours boasted of a wonderful civilization on the Banks of the Nile. . . . Ancient Egypt gave the world Civilization. . . . Greece and Rome have robbed Egypt of her arts and letters, and taken all the credit to themselves."[3]

From Garvey's Pan-Africanism slowly grew the dream of Africans from every country on earth uniting for a common goal: to deliver Africa from the Europeans who occupied it and to recover their glorious heritage.

Frederick Douglass was an important African-American leader
who believed in a common bond between all black people.

Meanwhile, Garvey called for justice for the immigrant West Indian British subjects in London. Again nobody listened.

In 1913, Garvey met Duse Mohamed Ali, the half-Egyptian publisher of *The African Times and Orient Review* in London. The periodical was devoted to fighting for justice for the native African and Asian peoples of white-dominated colonies around the world. Colonies are countries that are ruled not by the people who live there but instead by people from another country. Jamaica, for example, was a British colony.

Garvey and Ali quickly became friends, and Ali hired Garvey as a messenger. Soon Garvey was mingling with leading black intellectuals, many twice his age. An article by Garvey was published in Ali's magazine: "The British West Indies in the Mirror of Civilization: History Making by Colonial Negroes." In it, Garvey expressed a hope that would soon become his crusade—that blacks worldwide would unite to form a great new empire.

Garvey traveled across Europe, writing and studying. His association with Ali gave him the freedom and the opportunity to do this. He read *Up From Slavery,* a book by another black leader, Booker T. Washington. In this book, Washington urges his fellow blacks to work hard, save their money, and get educated. Washington, perhaps the best-known black man in the United States at that time, believed that the black race would rise through its own efforts, not by help from the white race.

Marcus Garvey recalled later that reading *Up From Slavery* changed his life. "My doom—if I may call it—of being a raceleader dawned upon me," he said.[4] Garvey read everything by Booker T. Washington that he could get his hands on. He was thrilled to discover that Washington had the courage to condemn British imperialists for the times that they killed Africans "simply because they [Africans] tried to defend their homes, their wives and their children."[5] Washington was referring to the times when the British government used violence to put down rebellions in its African colonies.

Garvey thought his own ideas were not that much different from Washington's. Washington did not favor having black people plead with the white community to help them become educated and economically self-sufficient. Instead, Washington said, black people must seize their own fate: Build black businesses that hire black workers. Build black colleges to train black youth.

Galvanized by Washington's ideas, Garvey realized he could no longer stand on the sidelines looking for allies. He made up his mind to take charge and make his great dream a reality. He hurried back to Jamaica, arriving on July 8, 1914, about a month before his twenty-seventh birthday.

4

"ONE GOD!
ONE AIM!
ONE DESTINY!"

n the ocean voyage from Southampton, England, to Jamaica, Marcus Garvey met a couple from Basutoland (a country in southern Africa now called Lesotho). The couple recounted their story of oppression and conflict with the Dutch people of South Africa, whites who had controlled the area until the British took over. "My heart bled within me," Garvey said later.[1] Out of those conversations, Garvey thought up the name of the organization he would start: the Universal Negro Improvement and Conservation Association. "Such a name I thought would embrace the purpose of all black humanity," Garvey said.[2]

"My brain was afire," Garvey recalled feeling upon setting foot again on Jamaican soil in 1914.[3] He was a young man consumed with his mission. Only seventeen days after returning to Jamaica, he founded the UNIA. The aim was "to establish a universal confraternity among the race," Garvey proclaimed.[4]

"The home of the Negro race is all over the world," Garvey said.[5] He became the president and the chief recruiter of the UNIA, calling on Jamaican blacks to "promote the spirit of race, pride and love."[6] The slogan of the new organization was "One God! One Aim! One Destiny!"[7]

Because this enthusiastic young man was the only member of an organization that he hoped would spread around the globe, he had a challenging task. He hoped first to unite all Jamaican blacks in a plan to use education and economic opportunity to lift themselves up. They would then be a model and an inspiration to the world. He thought independent black-ruled nations would rise up in Africa and welcome black people from all countries. Garvey believed in black government, black businesses, and total black control of blacks' lives. Only in that way would his people gain pride and success.

Marcus Garvey did not have much money with which to launch the UNIA. The modest membership fees raised almost nothing. Garvey traveled throughout Jamaica, supporting himself with his small savings from his jobs in London. He visited towns and villages to explain his goals. He organized lectures and debates, speaking contests, and entertainment in the hopes of drawing crowds. When he had even a small crowd, he would fervently explain the program of the UNIA.

Among Garvey's many allies in the UNIA was a young woman named Amy Ashwood. Born in Port Antonio, Jamaica, she had lived with her family for some time in Panama. She shared Garvey's vision of the future. She had met Garvey in Jamaica in 1914 at a debating club when she was just seventeen. She began helping to organize the early meetings of the UNIA in Collegiate Hall in Kingston and started a women's club devoted to the UNIA ideals.

Garvey fell in love with Ashwood, and they began dating in Jamaica. Ashwood's family lived in Panama and they did not approve of the relationship. At the time, Garvey's only income was from selling greeting cards and tombstones, and Ashwood's family regarded him as a poor marriage prospect for their daughter.[8] Garvey persisted in trying to win Ashwood. He sent her many love letters in which he addressed her as "My Josephine," and signed them from "your devoted Napoleon, Marcus."[9] He was comparing their relationship to the romance between the Emperor Napoleon Bonaparte and his love, Josephine, in France.

Ashwood's parents demanded that she return to Panama, but instead, in September 1918, she went to New York to see Garvey. She became his chief assistant in the New York UNIA.

Sometimes Garvey would carry his message to black church services, where the preachers would yield their pulpit to the zealous young man. Garvey talked about setting up adult education and vocational schools modeled after the Tuskegee Institute in the United States. Established by the Alabama State Legislature in 1880, the Tuskegee Normal School was started to train black teachers. Booker T. Washington was its first president. At first, Washington ran his institute in a donated shanty in Tuskegee. He raised funds for the school by traveling around by horse and buggy, asking for donations. Washington saw his little school grow to one hundred buildings and sixteen hundred students before he died. Garvey was inspired by this achievement, and he believed he could do something similar for his people in Jamaica.

Some white people in Jamaica who were sympathetic to black progress liked Garvey's ideas. The Jamaican governor attended some of his rallies, and the Anglican bishop of Kingston appeared at some of Garvey's social functions. Years later, during the civil rights movement in the United States, many white

The writings and philosophy of Booker T. Washington, above, inspired Garvey to work to improve the quality of black lives.

people would rally to the cause of Martin Luther King, Jr., and other black civil rights leaders. The same thing happened in Jamaica in the early 1900s as Garvey presented his case for black unity and equality.

Garvey's ideas were less popular in the nonwhite community for several reasons. The majority of Jamaican working people were not well educated. Garvey was very concerned about this. He said blacks "need a great deal of improvement."[10] Garvey had educated himself by reading everything he could, but most Jamaican blacks did not have access to large libraries or the opportunity to read books. They were generally not educated enough to understand Garvey's ideas.

Presenting even more of a problem for Garvey's new organization were the colored middle class (people of mixed African and European heritage) and the wealthier black people. They already had some status and felt that rocking the boat would endanger their own gains. "In Jamaica, the colored and successful black people regard themselves as white," Garvey complained.[11] Most of them were not willing to take part in programs to raise up the less fortunate.

"I was openly hated and persecuted by some of these colored men," Garvey said bitterly. "They hated me worse than poison."[12] The very dark skinned Garvey was viewed with suspicion by black people who were shades lighter. "I really never knew there was so much color prejudice in Jamaica, my own native home," he observed.[13]

Still, Garvey turned passionately to the black people of Jamaica for support. "Sons and daughters of Africa," he shouted at dozens of meeting and rallies, "I say to you, arise. Take on the toga of race pride."[14]

Garvey pleaded and nagged his fellow blacks to join the UNIA. As he prepared for the first convention of the UNIA, Garvey received word that his father had become completely penniless, with no means of support, and had been committed to St. Ann's Poor House. There had been little or no communication between Garvey and his father after Garvey's parents separated.

The convention was a modest gathering in August of about one hundred members, all of whom Garvey had recruited. He assured these blacks that the white people of Jamaica were eager to assist them in improving themselves. He told his followers that once the black people demonstrated a desire to improve themselves, all other races of the world would treat them with equality. The small UNIA group received the message enthusiastically, but Garvey had to face a hard truth: His cause was not off to a good start.

Most of Garvey's speeches around Jamaica fell on deaf ears. The black people of Jamaica were poor and hardworking. They were uneducated and ill treated.

They did not have the time, resources, or spirit to join Garvey's movement.

Reluctantly, Garvey realized that he had to change his plans. He had hoped the Jamaican UNIA would be a shining example to the rest of the world, a model of how black people could successfully shape their own futures. The island of Jamaica was too small for his grand schemes. He needed a different, larger stage on which to launch his ambitious dream.

Garvey wrote to Booker T. Washington early in 1915, and Washington invited him to visit Tuskegee Institute. In April 1915, Garvey wrote another letter to Washington, explaining his intention to visit the United States and "lecture in the interest of my Association." He added that he planned to do most of his lecturing in the American South "among the people of our race."[15] Garvey was hopeful that he could gain Washington's introduction to people who could help his cause. He told Washington he would be arriving in the United States "a stranger to the people," implying that he could use help.[16] Washington was gracious in his reply, promising to make Garvey's visit "as pleasant and as profitable as we can."[17]

Garvey was not able to leave immediately for the United States, and by the time he was ready to make the trip, Washington was dead. There would be no famous black American smoothing the way as he carried his mission forward in the South.

5

THE UNIA GROWS

n the chilly day of March 24, 1916, twenty-eight-year-old Marcus Garvey arrived in New York. The young man had never before seen such a large city, with hundreds of people crowding the streets. But there is no evidence that Garvey spent much time enjoying local wonders like the Statue of Liberty and the Brooklyn Bridge.

Because Booker T. Washington had died, Garvey scrapped his plans to begin his recruitment drive in the American South. Instead, he hurried to find work, for he needed money to support himself, to rent lecture halls, and to put out newsletters. Garvey was hired as a printer.

He used his free time to explain the goals of the UNIA from street corners. Whenever a few people gathered to listen, Garvey spoke with as much enthusiasm as if he were expounding to thousands. He urged black people to educate themselves and to unite through the UNIA to gain equality.

Garvey won followers in Harlem, a neighborhood with a large black population. After three months of persistent street-corner lectures, he had collected enough money in donations to travel for a year. In Boston; Washington, D.C.; and Chicago, he spoke to black people and listened to their problems. They had many of the same difficulties as blacks in Jamaica and South and Central America: prejudice, few economic opportunities, and low self-esteem.

As Garvey got to know the ordinary black people and black politicians of Harlem, he developed a dislike of the established black leaders, calling them "scheming politicians."[1] He complained that they "had no program" and were "living off their so-called leadership while the poor people were groping in the dark."[2]

Garvey was struck by the great problem of southern blacks migrating North in large numbers in 1916 and 1917. They were escaping the harsh discrimination and lack of jobs in the South, but in the North they were living in substandard housing and earning low wages. Most had little or no education. They were often resented by northern whites because, desperate

Harlem at the beginning of the 1900s was a bustling center for black culture.

for work, they worked for less than whites. Often, black workers were simply unwelcome in the white office, factory, and even service environments. Race riots and lynchings became commonplace.

Even though there was less legal discrimination in the North than in the South, in practice there was still no equality. Blacks could not live where they wanted; they were often refused service in stores and restaurants; and they were not hired for well-paying jobs. On the other hand, Garvey was impressed by the fact that, in spite of all the hurdles, some blacks were doing very well. They owned banks, stores, and cafés, and they lived in nice homes. He was cheered by this.

On June 12, 1917, Garvey heard a lecture by Hubert H. Harrison, a militant black man, at the Bethel African Methodist Episcopal (A.M.E.) Church in New York. After his talk, Harrison, who had met Garvey earlier, invited the young man to address the audience. Garvey spoke of his dreams for a united black population, and he was warmly received.

Garvey was so encouraged by his reception at the A.M.E. Church that he began asking to speak at other churches. He was welcomed, and his powerful, eloquent speaking style impressed his listeners. Many had never heard this message presented so forcefully before. "Hitch your hopes to the stars," Garvey cried. "Yes, rise as high as the very stars themselves."[3]

At a time when many black Americans were buying

products to straighten their hair so it would be more like white peoples' hair, Garvey shouted, "God made no mistake when he made us black with kinky hair."[4]

"Mothers," he demanded, "give your children dolls that look like them to play with and cuddle."[5] Black dolls were hard to find at that time, and most black children played with white dolls. Garvey believed this added to the low self-esteem of black girls, who saw in the golden-haired, blue-eyed baby dolls an ideal of beauty they could never attain. Skin bleaching was a common practice among black women as a way to be more beautiful. If a black woman looked light-skinned, it was said that she "passed for white," and this was considered desirable by many black people.

Marcus Garvey had a triumphant message that flew in the face of this cultural glorification of lighter skin. He boasted of his own pure blackness, insisting that not only was it not inferior to whiteness, but it was a badge of pride. "It is an honour to be black," he said. "Nothing is wrong with black skin."[6] He advised black people to hang portraits of black people who have achieved greatness.

"Organize as a race," Marcus Garvey thundered, "or perish as a race."[7] With that ringing battle cry, he organized the New York chapter of the Universal Negro Improvement Association in 1917, run by a board of elected officials. Garvey was the adviser to the

American UNIA, while remaining president of the UNIA in Jamaica.

Garvey ran into immediate trouble from the black political leaders of Harlem. They controlled other organizations in Harlem, and they decided to take control of the UNIA as well. They saw Garvey as an outsider. There was a nasty struggle during a UNIA meeting, during which the Harlem politicians grabbed control of Garvey's organization. Garvey and his friends walked out and established another chapter of the UNIA in New York. Garvey became its president, and New York became international headquarters for the organization. Garvey began calling meetings in convention halls.

Garvey wrote the UNIA's *Constitution and Book of Laws,* identifying the organization as a "social, friendly, humanitarian, charitable, educational, institutional, constructive, and expansive society." The purpose of the UNIA was to "work for the general uplift of the Negro Peoples of the World."[8]

Garvey outlined in detail how meetings were to be conducted, even designating the music and prayers to be included. He stated that all black people of the world, whether they knew it or not, were members of the UNIA, but only those who paid dues were "active members."[9]

Garvey also started the journal *Negro World* in 1918, using his own funds and some donations. *Negro World* was intended to spread the ideas of the UNIA and proudly pointed to the accomplishments of black people throughout history. Garvey edited the paper without a salary until 1920. He traveled around the country spreading word of the journal, all at his own expense. He was eager to get it into the hands of as many readers as possible.[10]

Negro World was given free to black households at first. Then the price was set at five to ten cents a copy, the same cost as other newspapers. Circulation in the United States, Canada, the West Indies, Europe, and Africa eventually reached from fifty thousand to two hundred thousand. There were columns in Spanish and French, though the journal was primarily in English. The impact of *Negro World* was powerful. Jomo Kenyatta—who in 1962 helped Kenya gain its independence from Great Britain and who was Kenya's president from 1964 to 1978—read *Negro World* as a young man and credited it with having a major influence on his life. Kenyatta later recalled, "In 1921, Kenyan nationalists unable to read would gather around a reader of Garvey's newspaper and listen to an article two or three times."[11]

Branches of the UNIA opened in Philadelphia, Chicago, and New Orleans. Garvey offered health insurance to members at a modest price, which made membership more attractive.

Marcus Garvey was traveling seven days a week to

spread his message. By the middle of 1918, he claimed 2 million members of the UNIA in thirty chapters around the world. (Garvey probably exaggerated this figure, but certainly the membership was substantial and the influence even more so.) The UNIA eventually had seven hundred branches in thirty-eight states in the United States. It also had two hundred branches in Central America and South America.[12]

In October 1919, Ashwood and Garvey survived a bizarre incident. They were in his New York office, an old brownstone house on 135th Street, when a black man, George Tyler, burst in. He had had a financial dispute with Garvey and was now demanding $25. During the ensuing argument, Tyler produced a gun and fired at Garvey. A bullet grazed Garvey's forehead, barely missing his right eye. Another struck his right leg. Ashwood courageously struggled with the armed man, spoiling his aim. Tyler fled, and Ashwood called for medical help. Garvey was treated for minor wounds. Tyler was caught by the police the same day and taken to jail. Garvey would later claim that the attack was part of a plot to kill him, engineered by his enemies. But the police concluded it was just a private feud. On the day of his court hearing, Tyler slipped away from his police escort and leaped from a jailhouse window, killing himself.

After the attack on his life, Garvey's popularity soared. He seemed to have just barely missed a martyr's death, and this added to his appeal as a man of the people.

Marcus Garvey married Amy Ashwood in a private Catholic ceremony on Christmas, 1919. Later that day, they had a lavish public ceremony with a grand reception. Ashwood was twenty-two, and Garvey was thirty-two.

Although Garvey and Ashwood were both devoted to the cause of the advancement of the black race, and though both would spend their lives in that crusade, they were unsuited to each other as husband and wife. After being married for just three months, Garvey filed for an annulment. (An annulment declares that a real marriage never took place.) Garvey then withdrew his request for the annulment, but in June he took his personal possessions from the home he shared with Ashwood. The separation proved permanent.

As Marcus Garvey and the UNIA gained more popularity, concern about the movement and opposition to it also grew. W. E. B. Du Bois, editor of the National Association for the Advancement of Colored People's journal, *Crisis,* conceded that Garvey possessed "singular eloquence," which made him "an extraordinary leader of men."[13] Du Bois saw Garvey's ideas as too extreme, however. Du Bois favored integration, not Garvey's separatism. The two men publicly criticized each other in the pages of their publications.

For his part, Garvey had deep suspicions of all black leadership. He had problems with entrenched black leaders in Jamaica and with the political establishment of Harlem. W. E. B. Du Bois had helped found the National Association for the Advancement of Colored People (NAACP) in 1909; he was an influential black leader. The NAACP worked to remove legal barriers to full citizenship for black Americans. Its legal work advanced black voting rights and gained blacks more equality in the courtroom.

Adding to Garvey's hostility toward Du Bois was the fact that he was light-skinned. Light-skinned blacks in Jamaica felt they were superior in some instances to darker-skinned people. This attitude had long been a thorn in Garvey's side.

"The NAACP wants us all to become white by amalgamation," Garvey charged, "but they are not honest enough to come out with the truth. To be a Negro is no disgrace, but an honor and we of the UNIA do not want to become white. We are proud and honorable. We love our race and respect and adore our mothers."[14]

Many people in the white community were also growing uneasy with Garvey's rhetoric. They saw him as a dangerous anti-American zealot who was teaching blacks to hate white people. By Garvey's strident pride in blackness, he was, in the view of some whites, inciting blacks to violence.

W. E. B. Du Bois, above, and Marcus Garvey fiercely disagreed about the best way to gain equal rights for black Americans.

In 1919, with the financial support of Madame C. J. Walker, a wealthy African-American cosmetics manufacturer, Garvey bought an auditorium on 138th Street in Harlem and named it Liberty Hall. Dubbed "a great zinc-roofed shed," Liberty Hall would soon hold nightly meetings addressed by Garvey and attended by thousands of people.[15] Other halls, also named Liberty Hall, opened in Philadelphia, Pittsburgh, Cleveland, Detroit, Cincinnati, Chicago, and Los Angeles.

That same year, Garvey launched what would be his most daring project: a shipping line run by black people. The Black Star Line was intended to be the business that would establish black people in the United States as an economic force to be reckoned with.

But the storm clouds of danger were beginning to gather over Marcus Garvey. The United States attorney general, Mitchell Palmer, had asked the commissioner general of immigration to check on the possibility of deporting the Jamaican as an undesirable alien. Already, *Negro World* was being banned in some parts of the Caribbean and Central America. The journal was considered dangerous because it gave the local black people rebellious ideas. The fears were somewhat justified. President Jomo Kenyatta had said of *Negro World* that it helped to nourish "Africans hungry for some doctrine which lifted them from the servile consciousness in which Africans lived."[16]

6

TROUBLED SEAS

In Cleveland, Ohio, in the early 1920s, the staff of an all-black barbershop—thirty barbers and manicurists—were told they would be fired and replaced by white people who wanted their jobs.[1] This was the type of injustice Marcus Garvey had been working to prevent. He believed that one of the major keys to black economic success was independence. Black people needed to own the businesses they worked for, and black workers needed black employers for job security.

This reasoning had prompted Garvey to launch the Black Star Line in 1919. The shipping company was owned and operated solely by blacks. Black investors from all over the world were invited to become stockholders and hoped the Black Star Line would become the largest black-owned business in the world.

Garvey also established the Negro Factories Corporation to build and operate black-run factories that would make the ordinary commodities needed by black customers. Garvey saw the rise of many new factories as a cure for the always high unemployment rate in black communities. He pledged not only that these new companies would provide jobs for black men and women, but that jobs would be waiting there for their children when they grew up.

The Negro Factories Corporation started and operated a number of small businesses in Harlem, including three grocery stores, a self-service steam laundry, two restaurants, a clothing factory, and a small printing plant. The corporation offered loans and start-up guidance to the businesspeople.

Eventually the UNIA and its corporations employed more than one thousand blacks in the United States. "Girls who could only be washer women in your homes, we made clerks and stenographers," Garvey boasted to white America. "We tried to dignify our race."[2]

The Black Star Line was Garvey's most ambitious company. Shares of stock, selling for $5 apiece, were advertised in black newspapers. With a sense of pride, hundreds of black working people dug deep into their pockets to own some of the new company. By September 1919, Garvey had raised $610,000.

The Black Star Line made such an impact that people began referring to Garvey's movement as the Black Star Line movement. Garvey boasted that the company became a world sensation and that "the news was flashed from one centre of civilization to the next."[3]

Once the Black Star Line was chartered, Garvey needed a ship, but he had no experience in such matters. Joshua Cockburn, who had been a lighthouse tender in the Royal Navy and had piloted ships from 1908 to 1918, offered his services. Cockburn pointed out that he was the only seaman involved with the UNIA who was capable of selecting a good ship and becoming its captain. Cockburn then chose a thirty-two-year-old merchant ship, the S.S. *Yarmouth*. The *Yarmouth* had been used for transatlantic shipping during World War I. It had also hauled coal off Nova Scotia and Boston. The Black Star Line paid $168,500 to the North American Steamship Company for the fairly small ship.

While Cockburn was readying the ship—which Garvey would later rechristen the *Frederick Douglass*—Marcus Garvey gave an important speech in Newport News, Virginia. On October 25, 1919, he told the crowd of his great plans for the Black Star Line.

The S.S. *Yarmouth* was the Black Star Line's first ship.

He promised "to float a line of steamships to run between America, Canada, the West Indies, South and Central America and Africa, carrying freight and passengers, thus linking up the sentiment and wealth of the four hundred million Negroes of the world."[4]

In November 1919, the *Yarmouth* set sail from the 135th Street pier in New York, bound for the West Indies. It had only a few passengers and a small cargo, but Captain Cockburn was confident. Garvey happily reported that "the white press had flashed the news [of the sailing] all over the world," adding, "My name was discussed on five continents."[5]

At the beginning of the voyage, the ship was listing—leaning over—badly, and the boilers barely worked. Cockburn would later describe the maiden voyage as "quite an adventurous trip."[6] Actually, while Cockburn slept, his vessel ran aground off the Bahamas, and the panicky crew prepared to abandon ship. Cockburn woke up in time and freed his ship from the snagged sand bar. Fights among the crew members and other mechanical problems also dogged the trip. Still, Cockburn rejoiced at the reception he received in Cuba. "People here are just crazy about the organization," Cockburn assured Garvey regarding the Black Star Line.[7]

By late 1919, the United States government had begun to investigate Garvey. Both black and white leaders had contacted the government with deep concerns about where the UNIA was going. Many of Garvey's critics believed his movement was driving the races farther apart and could eventually lead to violence. The Justice Department began gathering evidence. J. Edgar Hoover led the investigation.

Through the efforts of two black undercover agents of the Federal Bureau of Investigation (FBI), known only as P-138 and 800, Marcus Garvey came under federal scrutiny. (These two men were the first black FBI agents. Forty years would pass before another African American was hired by the FBI.)

J. Edgar Hoover, who later became director of the FBI, was a powerful and greatly feared lawman. He was especially concerned with Communist threats within the United States. Communism was the political system followed by the Union of Soviet Socialist Republics (USSR) at that time. Under this system, the government controlled the production and distribution of goods. Private ownership was not allowed. Communism starkly contrasts with capitalism, the system followed in the United States. Under capitalism, individuals and corporations, rather than the government, own goods and factories—and therefore they can benefit from any profits.

In the early 1900s, Hoover and many politicians were concerned that the Americans who favored communism over capitalism would try to overthrow the U.S. government. Hoover sent a memorandum

J. Edgar Hoover, who worked for the United States Justice Department, suspected Garvey of supporting the Communist movement.

dated October 11, 1919, to Special Agent Ridgely concerning Marcus Garvey. Hoover noted that Garvey was "active among the radical elements in New York City in agitating the negro movement," and he expressed regret that Garvey had not yet violated federal law because then he could be charged with "being an undesirable alien" and deported.[8]

Hoover believed that Communists working in the United States were trying to turn black people against the government. He cited the economic activities of the Black Star Line as a good place to look for evidence against Garvey. "There might be some proceeding against him for fraud in connection with his Black Star Line," Hoover said, ending the letter by suggesting that Garvey might be in favor of Bolshevism (Communism).[9]

In fact Marcus Garvey was bitterly opposed to Communism. He had written that it was "vile and wicked" for Communist agents to try to recruit black people to their cause.[10] Garvey denounced the Communists as cruel white men just looking for a chance to make a fool out of the black man.[11]

Hoover conceded that Garvey was a "fine orator creating much excitement among the Negroes."[12] He believed this was even more reason to fear the Jamaican. As Garvey continued to promote the UNIA, the U.S. government was building its case against him.

Prohibition—a ban on the sale of liquor—was

scheduled to go into effect in the United States in
January 1920. To beat the deadline, the Green River
Distillery Company rapidly loaded 4.8 million dollars'
worth of whiskey onto the *Yarmouth* for its second
voyage to Cuba. Once again, the old ship listed
seriously as it left the dock. Two days later, about one
hundred miles from the Cuban harbor, the ship began
to sink. The crew was drunk when the U.S. Coast
Guard arrived to tow the ship back to New York, where
government agents were waiting to seize the cargo.

After repairs, the *Yarmouth* made another effort to
reach Cuba with fresh cargo—and succeeded—but on
its return voyage in May, it ran aground near Boston.
The ill-fated ship made just one more voyage to the
West Indies before colliding with another ship in New
York harbor. Eventually the *Yarmouth* was sold for just
$1,625 when the National Dry Dock and Repair
Company sued for unpaid bills. In its brief and
disastrous career, the ship had cost the Black Star Line
almost $200,000 in lost cargo and repair bills. The
stockholders were remarkably patient in the face of
this distressing news.

Garvey then spent $35,000 to buy the *Shady Side,* a
small, fifty-year-old side-wheel excursion boat. It had
been used to carry vacationers on the Hudson River.
Almost immediately, it sprang a leak during an ice
storm and sank quietly to the bottom of the Hudson.

Next came the *Kanawha,* a converted pleasure

The S.S. *Shady Side* proved to be another big loss for the Black Star Line.

yacht that cost $60,000. Filled with passengers who paid $1.25 for the trip, the *Kanawha* cruised down the Hudson River as far as 206th Street. A boiler cover blew, scalding a crew member to death. After repairs, the *Kanawha* set off for Cuba, getting only as far as the Delaware River before breaking down. The *Kanawha* was eventually abandoned at sea.

All the voyages of the Black Star Line were sent off and greeted with fanfare. The one time the *Yarmouth* had reached Cuba, throngs of people appeared to shower the crew with flowers and gifts of fruits and vegetables, treating the crew as heroes. In Philadelphia, Boston, and New York, thousands of spectators cheered the ships off. But even on occasions when the ships reached their destinations, there was not enough cargo and there were not enough passengers to turn a profit. The trips were not a financial success.

Later, a bitter Marcus Garvey blamed Captain Cockburn for much of the failure. Garvey said that Cockburn "had in his hands the destiny of the Negro race on the high seas. If he had proved true and sincere the Negro race today would be regarded as a serious competitor in maritime affairs; but Cockburn deceived and sold me."[13]

In truth, Cockburn was probably not up to the task. He had no experience in selecting ships and paid too much for unseaworthy vessels. For example, just before Cockburn laid out $60,000 for the broken-down

Kanawha, a more shrewd buyer had been offered the yacht for $10,000 and turned it down. The Black Star Line was doomed not by evildoers but by inexperienced men.

As the Black Star Line was failing, Garvey blamed the white-ruled commercial world, which, he said, would not allow competition from a black-owned enterprise like Black Star. He also blamed "invisible influences that were operating against me all over the world, caused through the secret propaganda of other Negroes against me in impressing prominent members of the white race and their government that I was a bad man."[14] Still, there is no credible evidence that Black Star failed for any reason other than mismanagement.

The tide appeared to be against Marcus Garvey, but his greatest moment lay just ahead. He was about to preside over a spectacle such as had never been seen before by the black people of the world.

7

"Into the Limelight"

ontractors worked furiously to complete the renovations of Liberty Hall in Harlem by August 1, 1920. It was to be what Marcus Garvey called "a red letter day for the Negro peoples of the world."[1] At 9:30 A.M., at 120-140 West 138th Street, the convention of the black people of the world opened. Twenty-five thousand delegates had come from many parts of Africa—Nigeria, the Gold Coast, Sierra Leone, Liberia, West Africa, and Cape Town and Johannesburg, South Africa. They also came from the West Indies—from Cuba, Haiti, Jamaica, Barbados, Trinidad, Grenada, and the Leeward and

Windward Islands—as well as from Central and South America, England, France, and the United States.

The twenty-five-piece Black Star Line Band and the one hundred voices from the Liberty Hall choir opened the meeting with familiar black hymns such as "O Africa Awaken," "Shine on Eternal Light," and the UNIA anthem "Ethiopia, Thou Land of Our Fathers." Ethiopia is a country in North Africa, but Ethiopia is also the ancient name for all of Africa.

The opening religious sermon was preached by the Reverend James W. H. Eason, a clergyman of the African Methodist Episcopal Church. Eason was an enthusiastic member of the UNIA, and he traveled around the country recruiting for Garvey's organization. He addressed the delegates with these words from Isaiah 60:1: "Arise, shine, for thy light is come, and the glory of the Lord is risen upon thee."[2] That was the theme—for centuries black people had been in darkness, but now the light was shining and they should wake up and become the great people they were destined to be.

An impressive parade followed as the UNIA convention-goers moved from Liberty Hall to the larger facilities at Madison Square Garden, a distance of more than one hundred city blocks. About thirty thousand people lined the streets of Harlem to watch the procession. "The demonstration was of such as never seen in Harlem," Garvey boasted.[3]

The UNIA Convention of 1920 was a major accomplishment for Garvey and the UNIA. *Top:* The Harlem Militia stands at attention. *Bottom:* Garvey and other dignitaries watch the parade.

Four mounted policemen headed the parade, and the marshal, A.M.E. Bishop Selkridge, rode a spirited horse up and down the line of march to keep the parade orderly. Young men in striking blue uniforms with red stripes on their trousers formed the African Legion. Some rode horses and others marched with military precision, though they were unarmed. Following were one hundred Black Cross nurses in flowing white veils, long white dresses, and white stockings. They were not formally trained nurses but, rather, young black women marching as a symbol of the way black women nurture the poor and needy of their communities.

The officers and crew of the Black Star Line were followed by the women's auxiliary, the female counterpart to the African Legion. Other marching groups included the Universal African Motor Corps and the juvenile and adult Black Flying Eagles.

Marcus Garvey, wearing a splendid uniform and a plumed hat, rode in an open car. One spectator said, "When Garvey rode by in his plumed hat I got an emotional lift which swept me up above the poverty and prejudice by which my life was limited."[4] This was a common reaction from the onlookers. Among the crowd there was no laughing, no mocking the pageantry. It sent deep feelings of hope through the hearts of the crowd.[5] Last came the delegates, many carrying placards with such messages as "DOWN WITH LYNCHING," and "AFRICA MUST BE FREE."

By eight o'clock, fifteen thousand people were seated in Madison Square Garden and thousands more milled outside. When Garvey stepped forward to deliver the opening address, he received a five-minute standing ovation. He later said that it was this speech that brought him "into the limelight of the political world."[6] It certainly did not calm the fears of those who mistrusted him when he talked about "four hundred million Negroes . . . sharpening their swords for the next world war."[7] Garvey's violent rhetoric was flashed around the globe, and he later lamented that he never lived down that unfortunate choice of words.

Garvey also said that evening, "We are coming, four hundred million strong and we mean to retake every square inch of the twelve million square miles of African territory belonging to us by right Divine."[8]

The convention lasted the entire month. Anyone who contributed more than $50 received an African Redemption medal in bronze; silver and gold medals were given for larger contributions. Garvey was elected the provisional president of Africa, a government he considered in exile. There was no country called Africa then or now. The continent of Africa had many countries, so the title of president of Africa was only a symbol pointing to the eventual unity of black Africa.

Other UNIA officials received titles such as Knights of the Nile, and an official UNIA flag was chosen. It was a red, black, and green banner: Red symbolized

Garvey's passionate speech at Liberty Hall gave hope to his supporters—but it caused fear in some of his opponents.

blood already shed and to be shed for freedom; black represented the skin of the people; and green was for the lush vegetation of the African homeland.

The elaborate festivities aside, the convention did take some major steps. The document that was produced, the Declaration of Rights of the Negro Peoples of the World, presented serious complaints and proposed concrete remedies.

Among the many facts of life cited as unjust in the United States were the frequent lynchings of black people suspected of crimes. Too often when an African American was accused of a crime, a mob of white men would seize and execute him without a trial. The person was denied due process of law—a trial to decide guilt or innocence.

African-American citizens in the South were often being denied the right to vote. When they showed up at the polls to cast their ballots, they were harassed and threatened. Many simply gave up trying. Also, African Americans did not have the right to services on a first come, first served basis in the South. They had to sit on designated seats in the back of the bus. If a bus was crowded, the black riders had to give up their seats to white people. In all these situations, mistreatment was based solely on the color of one's skin.

"Our families are often humiliated and insulted by drunken white men who habitually pass through the Jim Crow [segregated] cars going to the smoking cars," they wrote in the document, citing railroad car abuses.[9] Black children had to attend separate and inferior schools, and black doctors were denied the right to treat patients of their own race in public hospitals. The document decried the refusal of many labor unions to permit black membership. From public drinking fountains to rest rooms, there was racial separation, with African Americans restricted to inferior facilities. It was an accurate picture of life for African Americans in many parts of the United States.

To remedy these injustices, the document demanded that fifty-four specific rights be given to African Americans. These included the right to equal pay for equal work, complete political and legal rights, and an end to discriminatory practices. It also asked that the word *Negro* (the term used for blacks at that time) always be written with a capital *N* and that August 31 be made an international holiday for blacks, to coincide with the date the convention ended.

The declaration was published, and some details of it were reported in newspapers, but it was not formally presented to any government agency, including the Congress of the United States.

Although the demands made in the declaration were not well reported in the press, Garvey's inflammatory words were widely noted. Garvey later said that because his rhetoric received such wide publicity, "France closed her doors against me in Africa; and

Italy and Portugal also and England became so scared and America watched me at every move."[10]

That same year, 1920, Garvey received word that his father had died in Jamaica. At the time, Garvey was devoting most of his energies to the creation of a black homeland in Africa, to which blacks could migrate if life grew intolerable in their own countries. There is no indication that Garvey returned to Jamaica for his father's funeral.

Garvey's movement began to be called the "back to Africa" drive. In truth, he never imagined that all the black people of the world would return to Africa. Rather, he saw the creation of a strong African state ruled by blacks as a way of exerting pressure on the world to treat black people with justice. On this issue Garvey said in 1921, "We are not preaching any doctrine to ask all the Negroes of Harlem and the United States to leave for Africa. The majority of us may remain here."[11]

Still, there was enough confusion in his speeches to lead some to believe he was advocating a mass exodus to Africa. This spurred some of his critics to see him as a foolish and dangerous dreamer who favored something that did not interest the vast majority of African Americans: moving to an Africa that they had never seen. Other critics eagerly misrepresented his views in the hope of making him appear ridiculous.

As a prelude to a black African state, Garvey sent a

In 1920, Garvey was named provisional president of Africa, a symbolic title that gave him no real power.

delegation to the black-ruled nation of Liberia to open the way for anyone who wanted to go to Africa. Liberia was a small country on the west coast of Africa. It had been settled in 1822 by pioneer American blacks sponsored by the American Colonization Society. In 1847 Liberia had become an independent black nation.

Garvey also contacted the League of Nations to ask that the former German colonies in Africa, taken from Germany when it lost World War I, be turned over to the UNIA as future black homelands. The league ignored the request. Liberian President D. King, who at first had been sympathetic to Garvey, then changed his mind. He had begun to fear that Garvey wanted to overthrow his government and establish the UNIA leadership in its place. The land in Liberia originally scheduled for Garvey's emigrants had been leased to Firestone Rubber Company, which planned to build a factory on it. (Firestone continues to play a major role in Liberia's economy, employing thousands of people and promoting the rubber plant as an important crop.)

In the spring of 1921, Garvey toured the West Indies and Central America, trying to raise more support for the UNIA. When he wanted to return to the United States, he had a problem: The U.S. State Department had declared Garvey a dangerous radical and sought to keep him from reentering the country. The department also advised other nations around the world to deny him visas. The order blocking Garvey's return to the United States was later withdrawn, but the incident prompted Garvey to fear that plans were afoot to deport him as an undesirable alien. To avoid deportation, he began the process of applying for United States citizenship.

The second UNIA convention was held in August 1921 under a financial cloud. Some disappointed stockholders in the Black Star Line were finally asking questions. The charge was never that Garvey was enriching himself at the expense of the stockholders, but rather that funds were being mismanaged. Despite these accusations, the second convention was as lavish as the first. The hall was transformed into a tropical paradise, and honors were bestowed on people who had helped the cause of black advancement. Some honorees became Knight Commanders of the Nile, and others received the Distinguished Service Order of Ethiopia.

During the proceedings, the chaplain for the UNIA, the Reverend George Alexander McGuire, formed the African Orthodox Church. He was an ordained bishop in the church, and some of his followers proclaimed that Jesus Christ and God were black. Marcus Garvey always insisted that God has no color. He pointed out that for a long time whites had depicted God as white, so there was no reason that blacks should not see God as black. "We shall worship Him through the spectacles of Ethiopia," Garvey said,

Like this Garvey follower in New York City, African Americans in the 1920s were drawn to Garvey's fiery speeches and compelling message of black pride.

adding, "God is not white or black. But if [whites] say that God is white, this organization says that God is black."[12] Eventually, the UNIA was to call Jesus Christ "the Black Man of Sorrows," and the Virgin Mary "the Black Madonna."[13]

Although stockholders in the Black Star Line had invested about three-quarters of a million dollars in the company without benefiting from it, Garvey appeared to be soliciting even more stockholders. This gave the United States government something concrete to use against him. The government had to prove that although Garvey was personally aware that Black Star was dead in the water, he continued to use the mails to solicit more stockholders. Such action would constitute fraud.

On January 12, 1922, Marcus Garvey was arrested on charges of using the mail to defraud investors. On February 15, 1922, Garvey and three other Black Star officials—Orlando Thompson, Elie Garcia, and George Tobias—were indicted on twelve counts of mail fraud. All four men were released on bail while the government continued to gather evidence for the trial.

The federal district attorney sent two trucks to the offices of the UNIA, the Black Star Line, and *Negro World* in search of evidence. They carried off books, files, and records, declaring that their intent was to get "everything connected with Garvey."[14] It was the beginning of the end for Marcus Garvey.

8

ON TRIAL

As his financial empire was collapsing and the federal government was building its case against him, opposition to Marcus Garvey from black leaders grew intense. Since Garvey's arrival in the United States, relations between him and other black leaders had been strained. He had been frustrated by black leaders in Jamaica, and many in America believed he had come to the United States with a chip on his shoulder. He denounced the "treachery and treason" of light-skinned black leaders, and he blasted the "near white" leaders of the NAACP. He called that organization the "National Association for the Advancement of Certain People," and he criticized the "venal, ignorant, and corrupt" Negro press.[1]

Because of the bitterness that existed between Garvey and the black establishment, many prominent black leaders demanded that the government investigate what they felt sure were financial irregularities in the Black Star Line. They kept urging the government to dig more and proceed with the prosecution of Marcus Garvey.

Garvey's bittersweet foe was W. E. B. Du Bois. In the beginning, Du Bois had mixed reaction to Garvey. In a 1920 issue of the NAACP's *Crisis* magazine, Du Bois had described Garvey as a "sincere, hardworking idealist" who was also a "stubborn, domineering leader." Du Bois credited Garvey with having "worthy industrial and commercial schemes," but faulted him for his lack of business experience.[2]

Over time, Du Bois grew more critical of Garvey, and Garvey's hostility also increased. Garvey called Du Bois "a lazy dependent mulatto" whose Dutch, French, and Negro ancestry made him "a monstrosity."[3] Garvey accused Du Bois and his friends of plotting the end of the black race through intermarriage with whites and dubbed them "the greatest enemies the black people have in the world."[4] Du Bois responded by calling Garvey "a little, fat black man, ugly, but with intelligent eyes," who was the "most dangerous enemy of the Negro race in America and the world . . . either a lunatic or a traitor."[5]

A. Philip Randolph, the publisher of *The Messenger* who later founded the Brotherhood of Sleeping Car Porters and Maids, denounced Garvey as an "unquestioned fool and ignoramus."[6]

In the midst of all this bitter name-calling, Marcus Garvey made what many consider to be the worst mistake of his life. He had always been fiercely proud of his black heritage and scornful of those of his race who were lighter-skinned than he was. But he carried this to an extreme by meeting with Ku Klux Klan member Edward Young Clarke in June 1922. The Klan was a notorious terrorist organization implicated in much violence against black citizens, including lynchings. Still, Garvey found some common ground with Clarke. Garvey treasured pure blackness and resented interracial marriages, which could result in lighter-skinned children. Clarke felt the same way about pure whiteness. Garvey appreciated Clarke's honesty in admitting how he felt.[7] Garvey further fanned the flames against himself when he publicly agreed with the Imperial Wizard of the Ku Klux Klan that the United States was "a white man's country."[8]

When an enraged black press denounced Garvey for appearing to join hands with the Klan, Garvey tried to justify his actions by saying most whites were hypocrites who professed tolerance while hating the blacks as

A. Philip Randolph, above, a powerful figure in the American labor movement, did not support Garvey's views.

much as the Klan did.[9] Stunning and outrageous as all this seemed to be, there was logic in it. Garvey did not believe the white and black races could coexist on a completely equal basis, and he wanted other blacks to see what he believed was the folly of their efforts at integration.

Infuriated black leaders who had always insisted that the United States belongs to all its citizens, and who fought for a future of equality for all, now turned totally against Garvey. Randolph's paper, *The Messenger*, adopted the slogan "Garvey must go," and he and other black leaders plotted against Garvey in earnest.[10]

On June 15, 1922, Marcus Garvey divorced Amy Ashwood Garvey, legally ending a marriage that had ceased to exist long before. A strong and talented woman, Ashwood had never been happy playing a role secondary to that of her husband. She felt equal to Garvey and showed it.[11] After the divorce, Ashwood launched a successful stage career in New York and then opened a restaurant and nightclub in London.

In July 1922, Garvey married Amy Jacques, another dedicated UNIA member. Jacques had been born in Kingston, Jamaica, to a prosperous family. Her father, George Samuel Jacques, was a widely traveled man who taught his daughter about the world and gave her the job of supervising the field hands on the family's plantation. She had the sort of upbringing and opportunities more commonly given to male children at the time. Amy Jacques had been educated at the all-girls Wolmer's High School in Kingston and was studying to be a lawyer when she visited the United States in 1917. She happened to hear Marcus Garvey making a speech in 1918. The twenty-two-year-old woman was immediately seized by the power of his message. When she contacted him, he made her his personal secretary and the office manager of UNIA headquarters. She was also named secretary of the Negro Factories Corporation and became Garvey's traveling companion. Garvey fell in love with Jacques during their political relationship. After their wedding, Amy Jacques Garvey devoted her life to her husband and his cause. Marcus Garvey had no more faithful and devoted person in his life.

In August 1922, a serious problem arose in the UNIA. During the third UNIA convention, the Reverend James W. H. Eason, the clergyman who had been a major force in Garvey's movement, broke with Garvey. Garvey charged Eason with financial wrong-doing in handling organization revenues, as well as disloyalty and bad conduct. Eason struck back by denouncing Garvey as an incompetent leader and a man without principles who was friendly to the Ku Klux Klan. A vote by UNIA members showed that the majority sided with Garvey, and Eason was thrown out of the organization. A month later, Eason founded a

Amy Jacques became Garvey's wife
as well as a key member of his UNIA staff.

rival organization, the Universal Black Alliance, further dividing the black movement.

Eason was to be one of the witnesses called by the federal government to testify against Garvey in the mail-fraud trial. On January 1, 1923, as Eason was leaving a church in New Orleans, he was accosted by gunmen and shot. The gravely wounded clergyman was taken to the hospital, where he charged that he had been attacked by Garvey supporters who did not want him alive to testify. Eason died of his wounds on January 4. Soon, two followers of Marcus Garvey, "Fred" Dyer, a forty-two-year-old longshoreman, and William Shakespeare, a twenty-nine-year-old painter, were arrested for Eason's murder. Both men denied any connection to the shooting, but both were found guilty of manslaughter and sentenced to eighteen to twenty years in Louisiana State Penitentiary. The Louisiana Supreme Court overruled the verdict the following year, and in a new trial both men were found innocent and set free. The Eason murder officially remains unsolved.

As Marcus Garvey's trial date neared, his enemies in the black leadership sent letters to Attorney General Harry Daugherty demanding a speedy and energetic prosecution. One letter, signed by eight prominent black leaders—including William Pickens, an executive with the NAACP; Harry Pace, a musician and president of the Black Swan Phonograph Company, which produced major black music; and Robert Bagnall, another NAACP official—leveled serious charges against Garvey. He was accused of trying to "spread among Negroes distrust and hatred of all white people."[12] A long list of Garvey's alleged misdeeds included his apparent agreement with the Ku Klux Klan. The letter also cited the Eason murder as evidence of violent elements in the UNIA.

For his part, Garvey saw the upcoming trial as "the result of a 'frame up' among my political and business enemies."[13] He later said that "traps" had been laid for him to be indicted and convicted "so that my career as leader of the Negro peoples of the world would be doomed."[14]

On May 18, 1923, the trial of Marcus Garvey and his associates began. While thousands of his loyal followers grieved, many others gathered in front of the courthouse to pray and offer support, singing hymns on the sidewalk. Judge Julian Mack, a white man, presided over the trial. The jury consisted of nine whites and three blacks.

Garvey immediately had a problem with Judge Mack, who was a contributor to the NAACP. Financial support for the NAACP included many white men who favored the integration of all races and who sympathized with the black struggle for equality. Garvey, however, saw this as an indication of bias on

Mack's part. He demanded that Mack disqualify himself, but the judge refused.

Garvey's lawyer was Cornelius W. McDougald, a respected young black Harlem attorney. But on the first day of the trial, Garvey fired him, believing he also supported the NAACP. Amy Jacques Garvey became suspicious of McDougald when he urged Garvey to plead guilty to a lesser charge and accept a modest penalty—a fine and a warning against such further activities. McDougald told his client that if the case went to the jury, "It will go hard with you," to which Garvey replied, "I will prove to the jury that I am not guilty of any fraud."[15]

Garvey then tried to represent himself, and this damaged his defense. He was using the trial as a platform to espouse his ideas, and he argued with the judge, who kept trying to focus on the matters at hand. Finally, even Garvey saw the folly of acting as his own lawyer. He hired a white attorney, Armin Kohn. Garvey was so suspicious of black professionals, whom he considered "traitors," that he felt safer with a white lawyer.[16]

The trial lasted a little over a month. The prosecution called thirty witnesses, mostly Black Star Line employees and stockholders. Company records were introduced to prove mismanagement and to try to show fraud. But fraud was not proved. The witnesses simply appeared to indicate that the Black Star Line was poorly run through errors born of gross inexperience. The managers seemed to have been doing their best, but they did not know what they were doing and the shipping line collapsed.

The prosecution's entire case was in trouble. The government's lawyers had gone through twenty-nine witnesses without proving criminal conduct. They were now down to the last one, Benny Dancy, a man who allegedly had been lured into buying worthless Black Star Line stock when it was clear that the shipping line was bankrupt.

Dancy, a janitor at Pennsylvania Station in New York City, owned fifty-three shares of Black Star Line stock. The crucial piece of evidence was a hand-addressed envelope with a stamped Black Star Line return address. Dancy had turned all his mail over to the federal government at the prosecution's request. He was on the UNIA mailing list and received not only stock solicitations but also announcements of upcoming activities. The key issue in Garvey's trial now centered on one question: Was the stock solicitation in that envelope stamped *after* the Black Star Line went under? Dancy admitted that he often left mail unopened, so he really could not say with certainty what was in that crucial envelope. He was a weak witness; his testimony was far from convincing.

At this point, it would have seemed that Garvey could expect acquittal, but the atmosphere in the

courtroom was charged. Rumors abounded that
Garvey's men were planning violence, and bomb
squad men and Secret Service officers flooded into the
courtroom.[17] It appeared that the case had become
less about mail fraud than the desire of the United
States government and the entrenched black
leadership to rid themselves of a man they considered
dangerous.

In his closing speech to the jury, the prosecutor
asked, "Gentlemen, will you let the Tiger loose?"[18] The
symbolism was clear: A man as dangerous as a tiger
had finally been cornered, and now it was up to the
jury to lock him safely behind bars.

Garvey responded to the prosecutor's insinuation
by saying defiantly, "There are millions of cubs loose
all over the world," warning that they were "determined to fight their way out of any corral."[19]

The jury convicted Marcus Garvey on one count of
mail fraud. On June 21, 1923, he was fined $1,000 and
sentenced to five years in prison, the maximum for the
offense. The other three defendants were acquitted.
Fearing reaction from Garvey's supporters, the police
hustled Garvey out a side door of the court.

Garvey's bail was set at $15,000. Garvey's friends
spent the next three months trying to raise the money,
while an appeal was pending. Garvey was sent to the
Manhattan Detention Center, known as "the tombs."
When he entered the center, he said, "I am not here

because I committed any crime against society or defrauded anyone, but because I have led the way to Africa's redemption."[20]

Amy Garvey spearheaded the drive to raise bail money. She later wrote that the leading bond companies refused to help when they heard who the prisoner was. Finally, the officers of the UNIA borrowed the money from organization members. Garvey was freed on September 10, 1923. Still awaiting an appeal, he immediately returned to work.

Garvey, undaunted by the disaster of the Black Star Line, made another effort to launch a black shipping company. He formed the Black Cross Trading and Navigation Company. Its stock was snapped up quickly by black investors who still believed in Garvey. Enough money was raised to buy the *Gerald G. W. Goethals,* a larger, more attractive ship than the others. The purchase price was $100,000, and another $60,000 went for refitting the ship. In January 1925, the *Gerald G. W. Goethals* left New York for the West Indies. Unfortunately, fighting broke out among the crew members, and once it reached Panama, the ship never returned. Again, Garvey suffered a financial disaster.

Amy Garvey had published the first volume of *Africa for the Africans, or The Philosophy and Opinions of Marcus Garvey* in 1923, and in 1925 she was working on the second volume. These were compilations of Garvey's many speeches and articles. Amy

Garvey had also become the associate editor of *Negro World* and campaigned relentlessly for a pardon for her husband.

On February 2, 1925, the United States Court of Appeals reaffirmed Garvey's mail fraud conviction. He surrendered to federal marshals in New York, who handcuffed him the moment he left the train from Detroit. On February 8, he arrived at the Atlanta Federal Penitentiary, where he said, "If I die in Atlanta my work shall then only begin."[21]

The movement launched so dramatically by the young Jamaican immigrant in New York City seemed to be ending in a dismal Georgia prison cell.

9

PRISON AND EXILE

In prison, thirty-seven-year-old Marcus Garvey was assigned to work in the library. He believed he was the victim of injustice, and he had contempt for what he considered corrupt government officials. A few other prominent men were also serving time at the Atlanta penitentiary: Indiana governor Warren McCray was in prison for embezzlement, forgery, and mail fraud; Mayor Roswell Johnson of Gary, Indiana, was doing time for a conspiracy to sell liquor when doing so was prohibited in the United States.

Garvey never complained about his treatment in

prison. In fact, he commended Warden J. W. Snooks, who, he said, "made everything comfortable for me."[1] When Garvey finished his prison chores, he wrote letters and poetry. He urged his followers to "hold fast to the faith. Desert not the ranks, but as brave soldiers march on to victory."[2] His most ambitious literary work was a seventy-stanza poem, "The White Man's Game, His Vanity Fair" (later retitled "The Tragedy of White Injustice"). Garvey had read extensively during his life. One of the books he admired was John Bunyan's *Pilgrim's Progress,* which chronicled the injustices against the poor by evil forces in the world. Similarly, Garvey condemned the evil oppression he saw used by whites against blacks the world over. Another Garvey poem, "Keep Cool," was later set to music as a UNIA hymn.

Garvey was visited in prison by many friends and supporters. He kept in touch with the activities of the UNIA. But his most important link to the outside world during his imprisonment was Amy Garvey. She traveled widely to keep the UNIA united and solidly behind her husband. She coordinated efforts to gain his release. She also wrote articles promoting Garvey's philosophy, which she fervently shared.

Amy Garvey was particularly annoyed by what she called the "would-be-white" sentiment in the black community. She called it a "slavish complex, the remnant of slavery to look like 'Massa' [the slave owner]." Amy Garvey had contempt for blacks who straightened their hair and applied creams to lighten their skin. She believed they should be proud of their curly hair and dark skin.[3]

Amy Garvey addressed rallies and directed letter-writing campaigns to gain her husband's freedom. Marcus Garvey himself wrote three letters to U.S. President Calvin Coolidge asking for a pardon. UNIA members sent telegrams and letters appealing for Garvey's release. In the summer of 1926, more than one hundred thousand people attended a rally calling for Garvey's pardon. Some prominent black leaders joined in the effort to free Garvey, including the highly respected president of Howard University, Mordecai Johnson.

Attorney General John Sargent urged President Coolidge to grant the pardon when he received numerous letters from the allegedly defrauded stockholders of the Black Star Line who denied they had been duped by Garvey. "None of these people apparently believe they have been defrauded," Sargent told the president. He added that they "manifestly retain their entire confidence in Garvey."[4]

The pleas for Garvey worked. On November 18, 1927, President Coolidge commuted Garvey's sentence, which still had about two years to run. But Garvey's petition for citizenship was immediately denied, and he was deported from the United States without delay as an undesirable alien.

Marcus Garvey was not even allowed to return to New York to say good-bye to his many friends and supporters there. He was taken from the Atlanta Federal Penitentiary directly to the Port of New Orleans and put aboard the *Saramacca,* a ship bound for Panama. The U.S. government was eager to get rid of Garvey as quickly as possible. Officials were not to release him until he was safely aboard the ship. Garvey was closely guarded by federal marshals every step of the way. Despite the government's haste, many of Garvey's friends had learned of the departure, and they gathered at the dock to watch him and Amy leave. Marcus Garvey stood on the deck of the ship, waving to the thousands who had come to see him off.

When the *Saramacca* reached Panama, the Garveys boarded another ship, the *Santa Maria,* for Jamaica. In Kingston, with his wife at his side, Marcus Garvey delivered a rousing speech and took part in weeklong welcoming festivities. Not everyone in Jamaica was glad to see him back. The Kingston newspaper, the *Daily Gleaner,* lamented, "It is with profound regret that we view the arrival of Marcus Garvey back in Jamaica." The editorial then soundly criticized the people of Jamaica for giving Garvey such a warm welcome, saying, "A new spirit has passed over the lower classes which has nothing to commend it except its

President Calvin Coolidge granted Garvey a pardon after an overwhelming outcry from Garvey's many supporters.

ignorance."[5] Neither the white nor the black elite in Jamaica had ever had much use for Garvey, and their feelings had not changed.

In Jamaica, Marcus Garvey did what he could to put the UNIA back together. Then he and his wife made plans to travel to Central America and Europe to remind his supporters that he was free, ready to pursue the dream.

The plans to visit Central America were dashed when the countries of the region refused to issue visas to the Garveys. They considered him as much of a troublemaker as the United States did. In April 1928, Marcus and Amy Garvey sailed for England. In London, Garvey contacted his old friends, mostly West Indian and African seamen. He gathered crowds around him in Hyde Park to listen to his speeches again. He sent letters to every member of the Parliament and to Protestant clergy whom he considered sympathetic to his cause. He urged liberal-minded whites and all blacks to rally around the UNIA.

Garvey established a chapter of the UNIA in England and rented Royal Albert Hall, a huge Victorian building in London that seated ten thousand people. When only a few black people showed up, Garvey blamed the hostile British press for turning the public against him.[6]

Garvey then conducted a speaking tour of France, Belgium, and Germany. French intellectuals heard him

After being exiled from the United States, Garvey and a few of his followers sailed to Panama on the S.S. *Saramacca.*

speak at the Club du Faubourg in Paris. After going to Geneva to renew the UNIA petitions to the League of Nations asking for African colonies, Garvey sailed to Canada. There, he made a speech urging American voters to select Alfred E. Smith, whom he called "a man from the people," over Herbert Hoover in the 1928 presidential elections.[7] Smith was the first Roman Catholic ever to run for president. Anti-Catholic bigots raged against Smith, calling him unfit for the office. Many of these people came from the South, the region Garvey knew had the most hostility toward blacks. Canadian officials were angry that Garvey used their country to meddle in American politics, and they expelled him from Canada.

Garvey returned to Jamaica and once again tried to launch his ideas from his native land. In August 1929, the sixth international UNIA convention was held in Kingston, attended by fifteen thousand delegates. Garvey presided over a grand affair, riding in a five-mile-long parade in an open car, wearing scarlet robes and a red-and-white hat. He announced that Kingston would be at the center of his future plans. When members of the UNIA in New York objected to this change, Garvey renamed his organization the Parent Body of the Universal Negro Improvement Association. This break further weakened the organization.

Garvey also turned to Jamaican politics. He formed the Peoples Political Party with an ambitious platform that called for a minimum wage, guaranteed employment, social security, workers' compensation, and improved working and living conditions for the poor. He proceeded to campaign for his ideas on the street corners of Kingston. The poor blacks who came to listen did not tell their white employers that they had become Garveyites, but at night they sang "Ethiopia, Thou Land of Our Fathers." They considered Garvey a hero.[8]

During his campaign for a seat in the Jamaican Assembly, Garvey severely criticized the local political structure, including the judges. He was arrested for contempt and imprisoned for three months. Effectively removed from the campaign trail, he lost the election. Later he was elected to a seat on the Kingston and St. Andrew Corporation, the governing body for the city of Kingston and the surrounding area, but the position was not important enough for Garvey's large plans.

During the years that followed, Garvey made Edelweiss Park, at 67 Slipe Road, Cross Roads, St. Andrew, Jamaica, the headquarters for his branch of the UNIA. There he produced a daily newspaper, *The Blackman,* and hosted an amusement company that put on concerts, plays, and dances. Garvey also headed a real estate and auctioneering enterprise. Modest economic success and personal happiness seemed to come at last into his life.

Amy Garvey recalled the best moments of that period. "Our first son was born September 17, 1930, and was named Marcus. Julius was born August 16, 1933," she said, adding that her husband, "was proud of being a father, but the work of the organization and financing of it came first in his planning."[9]

Sadly, the worldwide depression that was taking its toll on economies everywhere struck at Edelweiss Park as well. In December 1934, Garvey could no longer keep up the payments on the complex, and foreclosure followed. Edelweiss was sold at public auction, though Garvey remained there a little longer until he could make plans. With two children to support, he needed money for his family and his organization. He moved alone to London in 1935. Amy Garvey remained behind with the boys, planning to join her husband when it was possible.

In London, Garvey again became a fixture in Hyde Park debates and published articles expressing his ideas about the world situation. Garvey was especially upset at the Italian invasion of Ethiopia in 1935. White armies rolling across the independent black nation broke his heart. He denounced the Italian leader, Benito Mussolini, for bombing and gassing "innocent women and children of the civil population of Ethiopia."[10] When Haile Selassie, the emperor of Ethiopia, fled before the invading Italian army, Garvey criticized him for listening to white advisers. He blasted the League

Marcus and Amy Garvey's two sons, Marcus, left, and Julius, posed for this portrait in Jamaica in 1940.

of Nations for allowing the aggression to succeed. Though bitter at the fall of Ethiopia, Garvey defiantly predicted that the black nation would triumph in the end. "Ethiopia shall stretch forth her hands unto God," he said, "and Princes shall come out of Egypt."[11]

During his stay in London, Garvey made brief trips to Canada for UNIA conventions, hoping that having them so close to the United States would enable his American friends and followers to attend. Some came, but their number steadily declined.

Meanwhile, war clouds were darkening over Europe, and Adolf Hitler in Germany had begun a violent persecution of the Jews. Garvey had mixed feelings about Jews. Although he often urged African Americans to emulate the Jews as worthy role models, he blamed Jewish property owners and merchants for economic problems in the black community. Many poor blacks rented from Jewish landlords and shopped at Jewish-owned stores. When rents or prices seemed too high, resentment was directed against Jews. Poor people of all races often regard anyone with more money as an enemy, and when the poor of the neighborhood were all black and the property owners were white and Jewish, Garvey and many of his fellow blacks developed negative feelings about Jews. However, on the subject of Hitler and his treatment of the Jews, Garvey's position was clear. "The Jewish race is a noble one," he wrote. "The Jew is only persecuted because he has certain

qualities of progress that other people have not learnt."
Garvey linked Hitler's abuse of Jews to white oppression
of blacks, seeing these deeds as kindred evils. He
predicted that eventually "Hitler and his gang will
disappear."[12]

Saddened by Ethiopia's fate, beset by financial
problems, and lonely for his family, Marcus Garvey
faced 1937.

10

DEATH AND LEGACY

Marcus Garvey finally saved enough money to send for his wife and sons, who came from Jamaica to join him in London. Economic conditions were very tight. Garvey was publishing his magazine, *The Blackman,* and running his organization from a small office with only five employees: two contributing editors to the magazine, an English stenographer, Garvey's private secretary, and Amy Garvey. Marcus Garvey himself earned a salary of just $1,000 from June 1935 to June 1938. His employees made even less. Everybody was scraping by for the cause.

To spread his message and raise more money, Garvey established the School of African Philosophy in Toronto in 1938. Although the tuition was low, only eleven students enrolled. Garvey decided to turn the school into a correspondence-course based in London. He promised that completion of the courses would "prepare each man and woman for a useful career and sure success and prosperity."[1] Forty-two subjects were taught, and Garvey's philosophy was woven into everything. He urged the students to read constantly, and he gave detailed instructions on how to be an effective leader. He advised short, well-groomed hair and neat dress. He warned against extravagance. "Play the gentleman," he counseled.[2] He reminded them to work hard because accomplishment is possible only through personal effort. He also told the students to "pray to God to give them strength."[3] Unfortunately for Garvey, only eight men signed up for the correspondence course.

UNIA membership all over the world was declining, and Garvey had collected just $400 in his fund-raising drives in 1937. He and his family had very little to live on. Worse, the cold, wet climate of England was very hard on the Garvey boys, who had grown used to the climate of Jamaica. In June 1938, young Marcus fell ill with rheumatic fever, which was blamed on the fact that his room was not carpeted and drafty air was coming in. When the boy's fever finally subsided, he was left with a knee he could not straighten. The school doctor told the Garveys that the boy had to go to an orthopedic rest home in southern England, or else return to Jamaica, where the warm sunshine would heal him. Julius, the younger boy, was suffering from bronchitis, which was also blamed on the chilly climate of London.

That same year, in September, while Marcus Garvey was in Canada preparing for the eighth convention of the UNIA, Amy Garvey and their two sons went back to Jamaica to live with her mother. When Garvey returned to London, he tried to make arrangements to send money to his family, but there was never enough. When he could, he sent $25 a month.

Marcus Garvey would never again see his wife and children, though they corresponded regularly. In one letter, he wrote, "I shall not be returning to Jamaica. . . . In case anything happens to me I want you to know that I have opened [a] Post Office account at the West Kensington, North End Road W. 14 Post Office in your name."[4] Garvey wanted his family to know there would at least be some money for them.

Garvey was fifty-one years old when his family left in September 1938. In letters to his sons, Garvey said that the UNIA would care for them if he died. As it turned out, he was wrong. There was simply not enough money in the organization's treasury to support Garvey's family. Garvey's last handwritten note to his two boys was dated January 6, 1940. Later, as grave illness overtook him, he dictated letters to his secretary and with great effort scrawled *Dad* at the bottom.[5]

In January 1940, Marcus Garvey suffered his first stroke. It affected his speech and left him paralyzed on his left side. Weakened by asthma and two bouts of pneumonia, he struggled to regain his strength. His doctor told him to return to Jamaica, but he refused, seeing that as the final blow to the UNIA and all his dreams. Despite his condition, Garvey read newspapers and dictated letters, conducting business from his cottage at Talgarth Road in West Kensington. Friends would take him to Hyde Park, where he spoke cheerfully and waved from the car. The people did not know he was crippled, and he concealed his disability. He feared that seeing his condition would give hope to his enemies that the end of the cause was near.

Garvey's secretary, Daisy Whyte, and his Indian doctor were carefully nursing Garvey back to health when he received a terrible shock. Amy Garvey later blamed a black reporter, saying he had put out a false news release that Marcus Garvey had died.[6]

Soon, stories all over the world featured photographs of Garvey framed in black borders. Whyte tried desperately to keep these false reports from Garvey, knowing it would upset him in his frail condition, but cables and letters poured into his home. The doorbell rang ceaselessly, and Garvey demanded to know what

Toward the end of his life, Garvey was separated from his family. It was his hope that the UNIA would support them after his death.

was going on. When he heard the news of his death, he was stricken. He told Whyte that he wanted to dictate a statement refuting the reports, but before he could say more, he cried aloud and sank back onto his pillow, suffering a cerebral hemorrhage. On June 10, 1940, nine weeks short of his fifty-third birthday, Marcus Garvey died. Amy Garvey wrote, "The brave soul returned to his creator."[7]

Garvey's last request had been for his body to be returned to Jamaica, not left in this "land of Strangers."[8] Amy Garvey tried, with the help of friends, to fulfill the request, but she could not raise enough money. So Garvey was buried in St. Mary's Roman Catholic Cemetery in London. There his body remained until 1964, when the Jamaican government paid to have its native son brought home and reinterred at the Garvey Memorial in Kingston. Garvey was named First National Hero, Jamaica's highest honor. Later, Jamaica issued a postage stamp bearing Garvey's likeness, and two streets in Kingston were named for him. A bust of Garvey was built in 1956, overlooking King George VI Park.

After her husband's death, Amy Jacques Garvey became a contributing editor to the black nationalist journal *The African*. She established an African study circle in Jamaica in the late 1940s and published *Garvey and Garveyism* in 1963. She raised her sons with the help of friends. Her elder son, Marcus, wrote

Garvey's mission did not stop with his death. These papers were displayed in the window of the Marcus Garvey Club in Harlem, New York, in 1943.

articles in the 1970s echoing his father's themes. He wrote, "Garveyism was relevant to the oppressed Blacks of the '20s. I submit that it is equally relevant to the oppressed Blacks of the '70s."[9]

Black nationalist Marcus Garvey was severely criticized by most black leaders of his day, but the passage of time has brought new insights. Contemporary black historian John Hope Franklin described Garvey's schemes as "fantastic" and said their popularity with the black masses was a result of the desperation of these people.[10] Historian Benjamin Quarles saw Garvey's value in his ability to convince millions of blacks that they were somebody rather than nobody.[11] Nobel Peace Prize winner Ralph Bunche credited Garvey with reaching and stirring the masses of black people as nobody before him had done.[12]

In 1965, as he laid a wreath on Marcus Garvey's grave in Kingston, the Reverend Martin Luther King, Jr., called Garvey "the first man of color in the history of the United States to lead and develop a mass movement," adding that Garvey "gave millions of Negroes a sense of dignity and destiny. And made the Negro feel that he was somebody."[13]

The legacy of Marcus Garvey is seen not only in these comments made by important men and women, but also in the lives of people for whom Garveyism made a difference. One such person was Elma Lewis, born in 1921 of poor parents. Elma was three years old

While Marcus Garvey's views sparked great controversy, he is celebrated today for awakening the spirit of black pride. Here, Amy J. Garvey, his widow, stands with a bust of Garvey erected in Jamaica in 1956.

when she read a poem for Garvey at a gathering of black children. Her brothers were newsboys for *Negro World,* and she later became a member of the UNIA Girl Guides. She was moved by Garvey's enthusiastic shout of "Up, you mighty people, you can what you will!"[14] Those words were a beacon to the young girl. She attended Boston's Emerson College and eventually founded the Elma Lewis School of Fine Arts for classical ballet. As she worked with hundreds of children, she frequently echoed Garvey's triumphant cry, "Up, you mighty people, you can what you will!"

The legacy of Marcus Garvey can be heard in modern reggae music from Jamaica, where people sing "Rally Round" about Garvey's life. The memory of Garvey remains a vital force where oral music performances have turned the historic Garvey into a symbol of black struggle and triumph.[15]

Garvey's legacy persists in Africa, where he is credited with inspiring black nationalism. Kwame Nkrumah of Ghana, the first black African nation to win independence, recognized the debt his country owed to Garvey by naming the national steamship line of Ghana the Black Star Line. Perhaps more clearly than most other people, Garvey foresaw the end of colonialism and the rise of independent black states. "Africa is a country of the future," he said in 1935, predicting that the natives of Africa would "rise to govern as other men are governing."[16] Garvey did not live to see that happen, but he helped cultivate the soil for the seed to grow.

In the final issue of *The Blackman,* Marcus Garvey wrote to the black people of the world, "Let us not turn back, let us hold on, so that when the final history of man is to be written, there will not only be glory for others but there will be glory for us."[17]

CHRONOLOGY

1887—Born in St. Ann's Bay, Jamaica, on August 17.

1901—Apprenticed to printer Alfred E. Burrowes.

1906—Moves to Kingston and studies orators.

1908—Mother dies.

1910—Travels to Central America and fights for workers' rights.

1913—Moves to London, England.

1914—Founds Universal Negro Improvement Association.

1916—Arrives in the United States.

1917—Forms New York branch of UNIA.

1918—Begins publishing *Negro World*.

1919—Founds Black Star Line; is shot by George Tyler; marries Amy Ashwood.

1920—First UNIA International Convention held in New York City; Declaration of Rights of the Negro Peoples of the World is adopted.

1921—Tours Caribbean and Central America to promote Liberian program.

1922—Indicted on mail fraud charges; divorces Amy Ashwood Garvey; marries Amy Jacques; meets with Ku Klux Klan leader Edward M. Clarke.

1923—Convicted of mail fraud.

1925—Sentenced to Atlanta Federal Penitentiary for five years.

1927—Sentence commuted by President Calvin Coolidge; exiled to Jamaica.

1929—Forms People's Political Party of Jamaica; sixth UNIA International Convention held at Edelweiss Park, Kingston.

1930—First son, Marcus, born September 17.

1933—Second son, Julius, born August 16.

1935—Moves to London.

1938—Founds School of African Philosophy.

1940—Dies in London on June 10.

CHAPTER NOTES

Chapter 1. "No More Fear"

1. Willard A. Heaps, *Riots U.S.A.* (New York: The Seabury Press, 1970), p. 115.

2. Lawrence W. Levine, "Marcus Garvey and the Politics of Revitalization," in John Hope Franklin and August Meier, eds., *Black Leaders of the Twentieth Century* (Chicago: University of Illinois Press, 1982), p. 117.

3. Ibid.

4. Ibid.

5. Ibid., p. 118.

Chapter 2. Jamaican Child

1. Lawrence W. Levine, "Marcus Garvey and the Politics of Revitalization," in John Hope Franklin and August Meier, eds., *Black Leaders of the 20th Century* (Chicago: Univ. of Illinois Press, 1982), p. 106.

2. Judith Stein, *Black Moses: The World of Marcus Garvey* (Baton Rouge: Louisiana State University Press, 1986), p. 24.

3. E. David Cronon, *The Story of Marcus Garvey* (Madison: The University of Wisconsin Press, 1969), p. 6.

4. Ibid., p. 5.

5. Marcus Garvey, "The Negro's Greatest Enemy," in Herbert Aptheker, *Documentary History of the Negro People,* vol. 3 (New York: The Citadel Press, 1993), p. 393.

6. Ibid.

7. Cronon, p. 78.

8. Lawrence W. Levine, "Marcus Garvey and the Politics of Revitalization," in John Hope Franklin and August Meier, eds., *Black Leaders of the Twentieth Century* (Chicago: University of Illinois Press, 1982), p. 106.

9. Robert A. Hill, *Marcus Garvey: Life and Lessons* (Berkeley: University of California Press, 1987), p. 35.

10. Levine, p. 107.

11. Ibid., p. 108.

12. Ibid., p. 106.

13. Herbert Aptheker, *Documentary History of the Negro People of the U.S.* (New York: The Citadel Press, 1993), vol. 3, p. 395.

Chapter 3. Central America and London

1. E. David Cronon, *The Story of Marcus Garvey* (Madison: The University of Wisconsin Press, 1969), p. 14.

2. Wilson Jeremiah Moses, *Classical Black Nationalism from the American Revolution to Marcus Garvey* (New York: New York University Press, 1996), p. 34.

3. Ibid.

4. Cronon, p. 16.

5. Lawrence W. Levine, "Marcus Garvey and the Politics of Revitalization," in John Hope Franklin and August Meier, eds., *Black Leaders of the Twentieth Century* (Chicago: University of Illinois Press, 1982), p. 109.

Chapter 4. "One God! One Aim! One Destiny!"

1. Marcus Garvey, "The Negro's Greatest Enemy," in Herbert Aptheker, *Documentary History of the Negro People* (New York: The Citadel Press, 1993), vol. 3, p. 396.

2. Ibid.

3. Lawrence W. Levine, "Marcus Garvey and the Politics of Revitalization," in John Hope Franklin and August Meier, eds., *Black Leaders of the Twentieth Century* (Chicago: University of Illinois Press, 1982), p. 110.

4. Robert A. Hill, *Marcus Garvey: Life and Lessons* (Berkeley: University of California Press, 1987), p. 206.

5. Ibid.

6. E. David Cronon, *The Story of Marcus Garvey* (Madison: The University of Wisconsin Press, 1969), p. 17.

7. Ibid., p. 18.

8. Judith Stein, *Black Moses: The World of Marcus Garvey* (Baton Rouge: Louisiana State University Press, 1986), p. 32.

9. Hill, p. 358.

10. Stein, p. 31.

11. Hill, p. 36.
12. Levine, p. 111.
13. Garvey, p. 396.
14. Levine, p. 111.
15. Cronon, p. 19.
16. Ibid.
17. Ibid.

Chapter 5. The UNIA Grows

1. Robert A. Hill, *Marcus Garvey: Life and Lessons* (Berkeley: University of California Press, 1987), p. 36.

2. Columbus Salley, *Black 100* (New York: The Citadel Press, 1993), p. 81.

3. Elwood Watson, "Marcus Garvey and the Rise of Black Nationalism," *USA Today*, November 2000, p. 64.

4. Lawrence W. Levine, "Marcus Garvey and the Politics of Revitalization," in John Hope Franklin and August Meier, eds., *Black Leaders in the Twentieth Century* (Chicago: University of Illinois Press, 1982), p. 114.

5. Ibid.
6. Hill, p. 202.
7. Levine, p. 119.
8. Ibid., p. 206.
9. Hill, p. 436.
10. Ibid.
11. Levine, p. 120.
12. Ibid.
13. Ibid.

14. John Hope Franklin, *From Slavery to Freedom* (New York: Alfred A. Knopf, 1994) p. 358.

15. Roi Ottley, *New World A-Coming: Inside Black America* (Cambridge: The Riverside Press, 1943), p. 70.

16. Levine, p. 120.

Chapter 6. Troubled Seas

1. Benjamin Quarles, *The Negro in American Life* (New York: Collier, Macmillan, 1987), p. 195.

2. Lawrence W. Levine, "Marcus Garvey's Moment: A

Passionate and Perplexing Chapter in Black History," *The New Republic*, October 29, 1984, p. 26.

3. Robert A. Hill, *Marcus Garvey: Life and Lessons* (Berkeley: University of California Press, 1987), p. 38.

4. Wilson Jeremiah Moses, *Classical Black Nationalism from the American Revolution to Marcus Garvey* (New York: New York University Press, 1996), p. 248.

5. Marcus Garvey, "The Negro's Greatest Enemy," in Herbert Aptheker, *Documentary History of the Negro People* (New York: The Citadel Press, 1993), vol. 3, p. 399.

6. E. David Cronon, *The Story of Marcus Garvey* (Madison: The University of Wisconsin Press, 1969), p. 82.

7. Ibid.

8. Memorandum to Special Agent Ridgely, in William L. Van DeBurg, *Modern Black Nationalism: From Marcus Garvey to Louis Farrakhan* (New York: New York University Press, 1997), p. 33.

9. Ibid.

10. Hill, p. 297.

11. Ibid.

12. Memorandum, p. 33.

13. Hill, p. 55.

14. Ibid., p. 56.

Chapter 7. "Into the Limelight"

1. Robert A. Hill, *Marcus Garvey: Life and Lessons* (Berkeley: University of California Press, 1987), p. 39.

2. Robert A. Hill, ed., *Marcus Garvey and the Universal Negro Improvement Association Papers* (Berkeley: University of California Press, 1983), vol. 1, p. 644.

3. Hill, *Life and Lessons*, p. 40.

4. Lawrence W. Levine, "Marcus Garvey's Moment: A Passionate and Perplexing Chapter in Black History," *The New Republic*, October 29, 1984, p. 26.

5. Hill, *Marcus Garvey and the Universal Negro Improvement Association Papers*, p. 646.

6. Hill, *Life and Lessons*, p. 41.

7. Ibid.

8. Levine, p. 26.

9. Declaration of the Rights of the Negro Peoples of the World, in William L. Van DeBurg, *Modern Black Nationalism: From Marcus Garvey to Louis Farrakhan* (New York: New York University Press, 1997), p. 25.

10. Hill, *Life and Lessons,* p. 42.

11. Lawrence W. Levine, "Marcus Garvey and the Politics of Revitalization," in John Hope Franklin and August Meier, eds., *Black Leaders of the Twentieth Century* (Chicago: University of Illinois Press, 1982), pp. 130–131.

12. Ibid., p. 124.

13. Ibid.

14. John Henrik Clarke, *Marcus Garvey and the Vision of Africa* (New York: Random House, 1974), p. 101.

Chapter 8. On Trial

1. Lawrence W. Levine, "Marcus Garvey's Moment: A Passionate and Perplexing Chapter in Black History," *The New Republic,* October 29, 1984, p. 26.

2. John Henrik Clarke, *Marcus Garvey and the Vision of Africa* (New York: Random House, 1974), p. 196.

3. Lawrence W. Levine, "Marcus Garvey and the Politics of Revitalization," in John Hope Franklin and August Meier, eds., *Black Leaders in the Twentieth Century* (Chicago: University of Illinois Press, 1982), p. 134.

4. Ibid.

5. Ibid., pp. 133–134.

6. Ibid.

7. Elwood Watson, "Marcus Garvey and the Rise of Black Nationalism," *USA Today,* November 2000, p. 64.

8. Clarke, pp. 225–226.

9. Levine, "Marcus Garvey and the Politics of Revitalization," p. 131.

10. Watson, p. 64.

11. Judith Stein, *Black Women: The World of Marcus Garvey* (Baton Rouge: Louisiana State University Press, 1986), p. 151.

12. Robert A. Hill, *Marcus Garvey: Life and Lessons* (Berkeley: University of California Press, 1987), p. 57.

13. Marcus Garvey, "The Negro's Greatest Enemy," in Herbert Aptheker, *Documentary History of the Negro People* (New York: The Citadel Press, 1993), vol. 3, p. 400.

14. Hill, p. 85.

15. Clarke, p. 102.

16. Robert Hill, *Marcus Garvey and the Universal Negro Improvement Association Papers* (Berkeley: University of California Press, 1983), pp. 55–56.

17. Ibid.

18. Ibid.

19. Ibid., p. 103.

20. Levine, "Marcus Garvey and the Politics of Revitalization," p. 135.

21. Ibid.

Chapter 9. Prison and Exile

1. Robert A. Hill, *Marcus Garvey: Life and Lessons* (Berkeley: University of California Press, 1987), p. 90.

2. John Hope Franklin, *From Slavery to Freedom* (New York: Alfred A. Knopf, 1994), p. 359.

3. Amy Jacques Garvey, "I Am a Negro—and Beautiful," in William L. Van DeBurg, *Modern Black Nationalism: From Marcus Garvey to Louis Farrakhan* (New York: New York University Press, 1997), p. 57.

4. Judith Stein, *Black Moses: The World of Marcus Garvey* (Baton Rouge: Louisiana State University Press, 1986), p. 207.

5. John Henrik Clarke, *Marcus Garvey and the Vision of Africa* (New York: Random House, 1974), p. 261.

6. E. David Cronon, *The Story of Marcus Garvey* (Madison: The University of Wisconsin Press, 1969), p. 146.

7. Ibid., p. 150.

8. Horace Campbell, *Rasta and Resistance, From Marcus Garvey to Walter Rodney* (Trenton, N.J.: Africa World Press, Inc., 1987), p. 64.

9. Clarke, p. 264.

10. Ibid., p. 352.

11. Ibid., p. 365.

12. Hill, p. lx.

Chapter 10. Death and Legacy

1. Robert A. Hill, *Marcus Garvey: Life and Lessons* (Berkeley: University of California Press, 1987), p. xlix.

2. Ibid., p. 200.

3. Ibid., p. 203.

4. John Henrik Clarke, *Marcus Garvey and the Vision of Africa* (New York: Random House, 1974), pp. 338–339.

5. Ibid., p. 339.

6. Ibid., p. 328.

7. Ibid.

8. Daisy Whyte, "The Death of Marcus Garvey," in John Henrik Clarke, *Marcus Garvey and the Vision of Africa* (New York: Random House, 1974), p. 344.

9. Marcus Garvey Jr., "Garveyism: Some Reflections on Its Significance for Today," in John Henrik Clarke, *Marcus Garvey and the Vision of Africa* (New York: Random House, 1974), p. 384.

10. John Hope Franklin, *From Slavery to Freedom* (New York: Alfred Knopf, 1994), p. 359.

11. Benjamin Quarles, *The Negro in the Making of America* (New York: Macmillan Pub., 1987), p. 196.

12. E. David Cronon, *The Story of Marcus Garvey* (Madison: University of Wisconsin Press, 1969), p. 207.

13. Columbus Salley, *Black 100* (New York: The Citadel Press, 1993), p. 82.

14. Dick Russell, *Black Genius* (New York: Carroll and Graf Publishers, 1998), p. 182.

15. Hill, p. xvi.

16. Robert A. Hill, ed., *Marcus Garvey and the Universal Negro Improvement Association Papers* (Berkeley: University of California Press, 1983), vol. 1, p. xc.

17. Lawrence Levine, "Marcus Garvey and the Politics of Revitalization," in John Hope Franklin and August Meier, eds., *Black Leaders of the Twentieth Century* (Chicago: University of Illinois Press, 1982), p. 137.

FURTHER READING

Archer, Jules. *They Had a Dream*. New York: Penguin Putnam Books for Young Readers, 1996.

Caravantes, Peggy. *Marcus Garvey: Black Nationalist*. Greensboro, N.C.: Morgan Reynolds, 2003.

Halliburton, Warren J., ed. *Historic Speeches of African Americans*. Danbury, Conn.: Franklin Watts, 1993.

Lawler, Mary. *Marcus Garvey, Black Nationalist Leader*. New York: Chelsea House, 1991.

Internet Addresses

Extensive biography and text of UNIA documents.
  <http://www.swagga.com/marcus.htm>

Poetry, songs, selections from Garvey magazines.
  <http://www.boomshaka.com/garvey.html>

Writings, influence, interviews with followers.
  <http://www.pbs.org/wgbh/amex/garvey>

INDEX

Pages with photographs are in **boldface** type.